AF869600

MARKETING MAGNIFIER

MORE INSIGHT, MORE MEASURABLE GROWTH, MORE CUSTOMERS

ANTHONY MILIA

CONTENTS

This book is dedicated to the entrepreneurs, business leaders, and professionals who have stories, passion, and knowledge to share with the world.

To my wife, Christine. You stay positive in all those times when I need just a little more positivity. You always believe in me and make me a better person along the way. You give me stability and happiness. You give me confidence and courage.

For my mom and dad—thank you for always loving and supporting me.

PART ONE
ARE YOU KEEPING SCORE?

INTRODUCTION

If you're a business owner or executive who's looking to make better marketing decisions for your company, this book is for you. Everything here is designed to help you achieve better marketing results for your company. It's written to be an essential and accessible guide for markets, executives, and entrepreneurs.

If you're already a specialist in marketing, this book can help you optimize your strategies for the long-term. We'll discuss big-picture strategic questions pertaining to different target audiences, business models, and industries that your technical training may not have covered. This book can help you to advise your clients and make choices for them according to their specific needs.

This book is not a complete technical how-to. It isn't going to teach you how to set up a social media ad for your business, or help you create your company purpose, vision, or mission statement. It won't help you define your values or even create a business plan.

Instead, this book will teach you the questions you need to be asking to bring customers through your door. These are questions like "Who is my ideal customer?" "What's the best way to reach them?" and "How can I remove obstacles and add incentives to help them buy from me?"

This is a problem that presents itself a little further down the road when you've already got your business set up but are trying to grow and scale. It may also be helpful to companies who find themselves struggling for customers when they weren't struggling before. Changes in marketing may be the answer.

This book introduces perspective, actionable takeaways, and a road map for success through digital marketing that you can apply to your business. It won't teach you the nitty-gritty technical aspects of how to buy or design ads. But it *will* teach you how to ask the right questions to determine where, when, and how to make changes to your digital presence and optimize that presence to create the greatest possible return on investment for your marketing dollars.

Maybe you have some experience paying for marketing that does not work. If you don't yet, you probably will someday if you don't learn a little bit about marketing best practices in this rapidly changing world.

No matter what your past experiences, you *can* succeed with digital marketing—you just may need to change your approach. We'll teach you how to figure out *what* to change, and then test to see which changes are working. We'll shine the spotlight on ideas, stories, examples, and strategies to help you recognize if your ship is sinking or underperforming, and how to multiply your return on investment from marketing.

This book is designed to help you get the most out of your marketing team, and to recognize and avoid red flags that might mean your advertising dollars are being wasted.

As the owner of Milia Marketing, I've been privileged to work with hundreds of business owners, executives, and marketing departments over the years to drastically increase their sales, build loyal customer bases, and move sluggish merchandise. My talks and consulting work have educated thousands more.

My client success stories have included local, regional, and national brands ranging from new entrepreneurs and mom-and-pop shops to Fortune 500 subsidiaries. They've included medical professional services, e-commerce, manufacturers, retailers, and many other industries. All my clients have had just one thing in common: they knew that they could sell more, if they could only reach more customers. You'll read several of their stories here.

In this book we'll show you how to ask and answer several key questions using data to optimize your digital marketing. Asking these questions will allow your strategy to change along with consumer habits in this rapidly evolving digital world, instead of merely recommending which specific best practices work today.

We'll cover topics including:

- **How** to set yourself apart from others in your industry in your marketing (and **why** you must do this to succeed).
- **Why** you must see your customers' point of view (and the most up-to-date ways to do this as of this writing).
- **How** website optimization can make or break your sales (and how to test top options to determine which drives more traffic and conversions for your business).
- **How** to tell if you're successfully resonating with your target audience *before* you spend your advertising budget.
- **How** to connect marketing and customer experience to keep first-time customers coming back.

However, if you're a decision-maker who does *not* hold a degree in this field, this book is designed to help you ensure that your marketing team is doing the most important things they need to do to help you succeed.

No matter who you are or what kind of business you run, you *can* find success in digital marketing. Even if you're already enjoying moderate success but you want to grow more, I can almost promise you that this is possible. Very few companies adhere to all of the best practices we'll discuss here, and even—sometimes especially—those with a track record of success to date may neglect strategies that can lead to explosive growth.

If you're a business owner, marketing expert, or entrepreneur who's seeing losses or a lack of success in marketing, I strongly urge you to learn the best practices I've assembled in this book, and execute the strategies found within these pages. To assist you in doing this, we'll include links to interactive worksheets that can help you define your target audiences, find your unique appeal, and more.

My experience has been that *any* business can see success—or failure—through digital marketing, depending on how many of these crucial tips they are following.

If you are suffering from poor performance in your business, know that runaway success is possible. But brace yourself to make some potentially painful changes. If you're not seeing results, it may be because your existing marketing, or even something about your business operations, is broken. Here we'll cover case studies from a variety of businesses whose systems, online or offline, were unwittingly losing their owners huge volumes of business.

Making changes is never easy, but I promise you: it's so worth it.

Anyone can have explosive growth through digital marketing. You just have to know what to look for.

CHAPTER 1
UPDATE YOUR STRATEGY FOR SUCCESS

THIS CHAPTER TITLE may seem like a no-brainer. Of *course* everyone should update their strategy if they want to be successful. Yet updating one's marketing strategy too often falls into the "important, but not urgent" bucket on a business owner's to-do list. Because something always seems to be more urgent, more immediate, more pressing, strategy updates just aren't prioritized.

In many ways, this view is understandable. The job of marketing is to bring people through your door. That means you don't know how many customers you're missing out on, because they aren't showing up to make themselves known. It's not an acute pain, and the losses may not even be obvious. And unless you're in the business of digital marketing, it's probably not your specialty. It's not your craft. It's not your passion. It's not what you think about every day.

But digital marketing *is* increasingly essential for businesses today. With each passing year, more business is done online compared to in-person. And, perhaps even more importantly, digital marketing is actually *superior* to traditional marketing methods such as billboards, radio, and TV ads when it comes to revenue return on your advertising dollar.

In today's market, those who dominate at digital marketing, win. They see more customers and sales, increased online market share, and return on their advertising spend many times over. Those who don't often struggle and sink.

That's why it's important to have a digital marketing expert on your side. Someone whose job it is to be up to date on the latest tools, and to continually optimize your business's return on your ad investment.

The first step to success in marketing, of course, is deciding that the job has to be done.

My hope in this book is to illustrate precisely *how* digital marketing expertise can benefit your business. We'll look at specific problems that digital marketing can solve, and the precise techniques that can be used to maximize visibility and sales.

You'll notice that some of these techniques require a fine-tuned understanding of your specific customer and market to work optimally; that's where the help of an expert comes in. But I'll also share worksheets that you and your colleagues can complete on your own to show you exactly where your online presence could use improvement, so that you can feel confident that investing in marketing expertise really will yield concrete results.

This book is a complete primer on the ever-changing realities of the digital marketing world, and why the attention you pay to digital marketing could make the difference between runaway success and catastrophic failure. As the case studies we'll look at show, this holds true whether you're a tiny startup or a megabrand that's been in business for decades and result in more customers paying attention to your business.

How can you bring in more customers every single day with digital marketing?

DATA IS KING

King cheetahs are absolutely majestic. I had the privilege of meeting some of these ultra-rare big cats on a recent trip to South Africa.

These animals just *bleed* fierce, predatory instincts. Their bodies are lean and powerful, never wasting a single movement. Their coats are sleek and shining, with blue-back stripes like rivers of ink meandering across golden fur. Every schoolchild knows that the cheetah is the fastest land animal on Earth, capable of reaching speeds over 60 miles per hour on four paws to chase down and pounce on prey. To watch a king cheetah move is to know what it is to be stalked. To have one fix you with its startlingly amber gaze is to know fear.

The king cheetah is one of the most impressive predators in the world. Yet this powerful animal is desperately endangered, with barely 7,000 cheetahs of any kind surviving in the modern day.[1] How can this be so?

The cheetah is the best in the world at what it does. No animal runs faster. In the short term, no animal can outrun it. Yet the cheetah does not have a wide margin for error in its lifestyle. Running that fast is expensive: it eats up calories at an astounding pace. Some zoologists estimate that if a cheetah tries and fails to catch prey three times in a row, the animal will have burned too many calories and will die before it can try again.

This means that the cheetah must strategize. To survive, they must know precisely what kind of prey is most likely to provide a calorie-rich meal and least likely to injure them by fighting back. They must never get up to full speed until they are *sure* of a kill. Running 60 miles per hour for fun, or in hopes of eventually running into something edible, will kill them quickly.

Your business is like a cheetah. Your business may be the fiercest, most majestic, most beautiful animal in its industry; it still needs fuel to keep doing what it's doing. This is *especially* true if yours is a high-performance business that pours tremendous time and skill into its product and sells to customers at an accessible price.

Such businesses don't have a large margin for error, either. They need a constant flow of revenue, and revenue can only come from customers. Thus, like the cheetah, even the most high-performing business in the world is in danger of extinction if it tries and *fails* to procure customers too frequently.

Marketing—*good* marketing—is the fuel for your business.

In the modern market, "good" means targeted. It means knowing precisely where your customers are and how to bring them in. It means not pouring cash into marketing until *after* you've answered the questions we'll cover in this book. Questions like:

1. What is the best way to reach my customer? The vast majority of entertainment, education, and social connection is now mediated digitally. Where is my customer spending their time and attention? What social media platforms are they using? What streaming services? What else? The answers will vary based on the demographics, personality, and specific interests of your ideal customers.
2. How can I catch their attention without annoying them, or getting lost in the crowd? How can I make my story about *them*, and make it uniquely suited to my customers compared to all the different ads out there?
3. Which types of ads are bringing in the highest return on investment? Have I tested different ad designs and platforms before deciding which approach to dedicate my whole marketing budget to?
4. Can I measure the performance of our marketing? If so, how? What metrics can I look at to know how well it's working?
5. Am I getting at least a 3:1 return on the advertising dollars I spend? If I'm not seeing at least $3 to $6 in revenue for every $1 I spend on advertising, how can we fix that?
6. Do I understand my customer's pain points and their experience of the buying process? Do I have clear messaging that speaks their language, and makes it convenient for them to buy from me?

In the pages to come, we'll discuss these questions, and how to answer them, in more detail. Our goal will be to absolutely optimize your return on investment on marketing spend. To assemble this book, I've interviewed experts and assembled case studies of fallen giants and unexpected runaway success for your benefit. I'll discuss how the fallen giants failed to adapt to changing markets, and how nobodies with virtually no investment capital became big names with the help of excellent marketing.

What works in this modern savanna, and what doesn't?

NOT TOO BIG TO FAIL, NOT TOO SMALL TO WIN

Just a decade or two ago, Blockbuster was *the* household name in home entertainment. They were an institution. It seemed impossible that they could ever fail. Yet today, only a single Blockbuster location remains operational. Die-hard fans of the VHS tape treat it as a sort of shrine to a bygone era.

Blockbuster *could* have gotten in on the delivered-to-your-door experience of early Netflix and outcompeted that startup when it was still in its infancy. It *could* have gone on to dominate streaming services the same way Netflix does today. But it didn't. Why? It didn't see how the world was changing. It didn't ask the right questions to see where the future lay.

Around Blockbuster, the world had changed. The rise of the internet allowed these bold startups to do things that the giants of yesterday had never regarded as possible, let alone necessary. Companies like Amazon and Boxed.com were able to use advancing technology to:

1. Gather highly personalized data about customers based on their browsing habits.
2. Create ads tailored to individuals, based on their browsing habits—then interject these ads into customers' daily experiences with entertainment and education.
3. Use advancing technology to coordinate the delivery of said products *right to the customer's front door*, virtually eliminating the inconvenience and effort required to go out in the car, physically find a store, and then find the specific desired product within that store.

Is it any wonder that the big-box stores of the past couldn't compete?

Of course, the physical store still has an important place within our economy. But the perceived purpose of these stores has changed. Once essentially glorified warehouses, with online ordering capabilities removing the necessity of physically picking up items, customers are still happy to pay for physical spaces—provided those spaces offer perks they *can't* get from delivery, such as:

1. A warm, friendly community space with warm, friendly, personable staff.
2. Education for customers who may be new to the industry, requiring staff who are not only warm and personable but also extremely knowledgeable.
3. Perks such as snacks, drinks, or a pleasant atmosphere that make visiting the physical space its own reward.

The shift away from simple procurement and into physical retail spaces as community spaces is one that many businesses are still catching up with. Some retailers are experimenting with offering memberships, in which ongoing subscription fees for access to the business's spaces and communities may end up turning more revenue than the profits on the sales of physical products.

While Sam's Club and Costco have used this model for decades, a growing number of retailers across industries have now begun to adopt the same model. From Barnes & Noble's new membership option to Rihanna's Savage X Fenty lingerie line, businesses are moving to membership models to encourage customer loyalty and optimize cash flow. These retailers who recognize how the digital era is changing customers' desires will be those that succeed.

Now that we've seen why so many of the giants of the past have failed, let's take a look at a story of a one-time startup who found runaway success by finding a target market and offering that extra touch of warmth and community that customers couldn't find anywhere else:

BOXED.COM: THE ONLINE RETAILER THAT CARES

I had the privilege of meeting Chieh Huang, founder and CEO of Boxed.com, at BizCon in Cleveland one year. We bonded over our shared origins as scrappy startups who began our businesses out of our homes. Both of us dealt with skepticism from friends and family who didn't fully understand our business model or, frankly, expect it to work.

Huang began his startup in his parents' garage. His goal was to compete with Amazon and Sam's Club by offering customers wholesale rates on products they could order online.

A guy who started in his parents' garage with a few tables' worth of shelf space wanted to compete with Amazon and Sam's Club. Sounds crazy, right? Yet in less than a decade, Boxed.com became a multimillion-dollar business with a fiercely loyal customer base.[2]

How did they do it? What did they offer that even Amazon and Sam's Club, with their seemingly bottomless budgets, did not?

The answer lies in two strategies that we mentioned earlier: precise targeting of customers, and the value adds of warmth, personalized experience, and convenience.

TAKING ON AMAZON

Huang realized early on that his status as a startup gave him something that Amazon and Sam's Club no longer had in 2013. He had the chance to design his entire sales, logistics, and technical support process from the ground up to yield surprisingly stellar customer experiences. By building his business on protocols that were designed to get to know and pay personal, caring attention to each individual customer, he offered a degree of care and attention that was unrivaled in his industry.

One of Huang's first innovations was in his logistics supply line. As soon as a customer's order was placed, an automated process immediately boxed and addressed their order and placed the addressed box on a conveyor belt. Maybe not all that different from Amazon, except for one thing: this conveyor belt had a camera on it. As soon as the customer's order rolled past this camera on the conveyor belt, the system sent a photo of the box to the customer's specified contact method.

The result? Often within minutes or hours of ordering, customers would receive a photograph of their package with a cheerful notification that "your box took a selfie." Talk about feeling cared for!

Huang built the same principle of customer care right into his protocols for all his customer service employees. Whenever customers communicated with phone support or sales staff, the salespeople were encouraged to be as friendly and personable as possible. They would ask how you were doing; they would sympathize or congratulate you as appropriate. And, most revolutionary of all, notes about the customer's life *became part of their permanent record with the company.* Boxed.com's IT infrastructure specifically provided spaces for customer care workers to make notes about the customers' personal lives in the system, and *these notes would be used* in future orders.

Like many companies, Boxed.com had a designated budget to give away freebies to build customer loyalty. But unlike its competitors, these were not random giveaways determined by partnerships between businesses. Instead, Boxed.com's gifts were based on the company's personal interactions with the customer. Mention that you've got two cats? Your next package may well contain a couple of free cat toys and a friendly note wishing your cat a great recovery from their vet visit. Mention that it's someone's birthday? You may receive a belated birthday gift for them from the company with your next order.

With this level of care and attention, it was possible for Boxed.com to provide an experience unlike any offered by megacorporations. Their prices may have been comparable to big-box competitors and their selection may have been smaller at first, but only Boxed.com could offer the experience of warmth and community because only they had taken advantage of advancing data capabilities to build personal relationships and care into their customer service process from the ground up.

Of course, making this business model work also required other, behind-the-scenes innovations. Boxed.com is also known as one of the most eco-friendly online shipping companies due to its hyper-optimization of automated packaging techniques and delivery route planning using advances in data capabilities similar to those that allow their personalized approach to customer service. These optimizations save the company money on shipping costs, allowing them to keep prices low—and saving on energy and fuel with hyper-efficient methods has the happy side effect of reducing the company's customer footprint.

Since warm, supportive relationships with customers are so important to Boxed.com's brand, the company also has to maintain warm, supportive relationships with its human employees. Affection is hard to fake, after all, and overworked or underpaid employees are less likely to be happy to talk to customers. This gives Boxed.com acute motivation to become a leader in employee support and workplace culture, since the company's leadership knows that happy, cared-for—or unhappy, neglected—employees pass their moods directly on to customers during the interactions on which their brand is built.

Now, all this probably sounds absolutely stellar. Chieh Huang used strategy to build absolutely everything in his company to be optimized for the changing market he was entering. But how was it achieved? How did he know exactly what to do to start eating up chunks of Amazon's market share at a time when the giants of the twentieth century were falling before its might?

Well, Huang's secret was that he knew the power of data.

DATA, NOT INTUITION

Sometimes, rarely, intuition provides an incandescent brilliance that hard data analysis cannot. The human brain is a remarkable computer.

The problem is, the human brain *can only analyze the data that it has.* And when the only data we take seriously is our own personal life experience, that intuition can leave us stranded in the past.

This is what caused the downfall of Blockbuster. Their leadership had powerful *intuition* about how to run their companies. The problem was, that intuition was based on decades of operating a company before the internet, before Amazon, before Facebook or smartphones or targeted ads. That intuition told the leadership of yesterday's giants exactly what had worked well—decades before, when *nobody* could offer the kinds of capabilities that Amazon and Boxed.com had harnessed.

In creating Boxed.com, Chieh Huang researched exactly what was working, and what wasn't working as well as it could, in existing ecommerce companies. He identified their major gain points and their major loss points. Many of these principles generalize to other industries and business models as well, such as:

1. Focus, focus, focus. Huang realized he could offer lower prices if he *only* offered large, warehouse-sized packages of goods instead of adding a tremendous amount of labor to the chain by selling individually packaged goods.
2. Optimize tech, automation, and efficiency. These are key points where speed, ease, and convenience can be increased, while costs and opportunities for error can be minimized. The sooner such variables are considered and planned for, the less cost in terms of time, money, and effort the implementation will require.
3. The gains from his focus and automation are passed onto his employees. Huang pays for his employees' children's college tuition and pays for the weddings of employees who have been with the company for a long time.[3] This creates a standard of living and security for Huang's workers that leaves them highly motivated to serve customers, solve problems, and see the company succeed.

Whatever industry you're in, the above principles probably apply to you. Developing your products and services based on data about demand and marketing nearly always creates better results than attempting to serve *everyone*. Automating as much as possible nearly always saves on labor and leads to less stressed employees and more revenue to spend on them. Happier employees almost always do vastly superior work and are much more likely to solve problems management may not even be aware of on their own.

You may be thinking to yourself, *Anthony, you said this was going to be a marketing book. This is about operations.*

Well, you're half right. On one hand, much of the above is more about operations and marketing. On the other hand, price-setting and customer service are two important components of marketing. If you can advertise that your employees and customers are happy, that's always a good thing.

But I'm also demonstrating some broader principles here. The same research and data analysis techniques Huang used to build his business model from the ground up *can also be used to optimize your marketing*. We're going to talk about that now.

The principles above are likely universal to all industries and business models, but there are also realities that are specific to particular customer bases and businesses. Today's data-driven world has allowed us to go beyond even basic demographic and industry targeting to provide hyper-targeted ads and services, just like Huang's hyper-personalized customer service. And that is something that your business should very, very much be doing if you want to optimize your profit margins and your return on investment on your marketing dollars.

Let's see how targeting a specific, ideal customer worked for one business from my hometown.

CHAPTER 2
DATA, DATA, DATA

DR. DANIEL IS the owner of a dentist's office in my hometown of Cleveland. He'd worked hard for years to earn his degree in dentistry and create a dental clinic in his home neighborhood. He strived to pay personal attention to his customers and make sure they got the care they needed. There was just one problem: customers weren't coming through the door.

Like so many business owners, Dr. Daniel had assumed that people would naturally flock to new businesses, as long as they were visible from the road. When that didn't happen, he despaired of how a small business owner like himself could compete with the marketing of more established dental practices.

When I met him, Dr. Daniel had a small cadre of long-time patients. These were people who had met him in his business's early days and given him a chance. But while neighboring dental practices sprung up and grew, he was struggling to attract new clients. He was running ads in the local newspaper and even on the ratio, but no one was responding to them. With the high operating expenses of running a dental practice, this was on track to become a huge problem very fast.

It hurt to sit down, look at his monthly bills, and realize he was barely breaking even after expenses. He'd worked so hard for this, and he *knew* he provided great care for his patients. Dr. Daniel had done everything right.

Hadn't he?

When I worked with Dr. Daniel, we discovered changes to his marketing strategy that increased his foot traffic drastically. But to get there, he had to give up some old beliefs he'd held about who was going to walk into his clinic, and why. How did we determine what needed to change, and ultimately make those changes happen?

To do this, he had to ask questions like…

WHO IS MY COMPANY BEST-POSITIONED TO SERVE?

Digital marketing is competitive. Like, really, really competitive. When global megacorporations and dozens of local businesses offering the same service can compete directly with you for your target audience's screen time, how can you stand out?

One way is to do what Huang did: hyperspecialize. While it may seem counterintuitive to "restrict" yourself to only customers who want industrial-sized cartons of toilet paper, for example, by offering *that specific product* you will be able to outprice competitors who try to diversify more. And by *marketing to people who need that specific product,* you will be able to make yourself more appealing to them than competitors who advertise to "everyone." Many people who are new to business and marketing fall prey to the instinct to advertise to "everyone." But to a marketing expert, "my product is for everyone" translates as "I don't know who actually wants my product, and that's why my return on marketing investment is pretty dismal."

To make sales, you don't want to offer a product "for everyone." You want to offer a product that is made *specifically for your ideal customer.* Your solution solves their problem or pain point. And it's better suited to do so than the competing products.

Consider this: if you were to read an ad that suggested an advertising solution described as being *specifically for* business owners of your age and gender who worked in your industry, how likely would you be to click on that ad? You'd probably at least be curious to learn why this ad claimed to be ideal for such a specific group of people.

Anyone can say they have "the best advertising solution," but an ad that openly claims to be "the best advertising solution for furniture store owners in their thirties" raises curiosity, at least.

The approach we came up with for Dr. Daniels was a little more subtle than that, but just as targeted. And it worked like a dream.

To determine who Dr. Daniel's ideal customers were and reach them in their daily lives, we looked at the following factors:

1. Targeting. Who is most likely to have the highest customer value for you? For dentists, women who are starting or have recently started families and who may not already have a dentist are the most likely to refer the largest number of long-lasting customers over time.
2. Up-front investment. The amount you spend on ads and the amount of time you spend fulfilling orders for deeply discounted products should always be *sustainable* for your business. But a well-designed ad campaign or offer doesn't need to be immediately profitable within a month of service and may even be a "loss leader" that sells at a slight loss, but gets people through the door where they and their friends end up spending many times the cost of the initial item that appealed to them.
3. Lifetime customer value. Remember to take into account the long-term effects of bringing in new customers from this group. Accounting for *just* the short-term value of the specific sale being advertised will sell your practice drastically short. It's the effortless sales happening six months, two years, or 10 years out that will really add up.
4. Referral strategies. Considering how to promote the referral of your business using your special offer multiplies the value of every ad. This is why you see so many "refer a friend and get $10" ads these days; almost every business with a lifetime customer value of significantly more than $10 profits from stacking these ads on top of other promotions, so almost everyone uses them.
5. Referrals can also be maximized by targeting groups (like

bridal parties) and people who are likely to be friends or family members of the people in the demographic group most profitable to you. This can also be seen in strategies such as targeting ads for men's products toward *women* who may wish to gift them to their men. Statistically, women are more likely to purchase certain classes of products and to spend more on them over a lifetime, so advertising these to women as gifts for men may make more sense than targeting men directly in some cases. This is the value of data.

When asking your targeting questions, there are both internal and external questions to ask. I recommend beginning by reflecting on the internal questions, and then *vetting them through hard data collection:*

1. Internal question: are there particular problems we're suited to solve due to our own unique backgrounds and experiences?
2. Data-driven question: who is buying our product the most *right now*? It's a good idea to calculate this in terms of *total revenue*, not total number of customers. You might find that one demographic makes up a majority of your customers by headcount, but another demographic makes up the majority of your *sales* through large or repeat purchases.
3. You'll get your best return on marketing investment by focusing on marketing to people who are similar to your customers with the highest lifetime spend (we'll discuss how to make this calculation later in the book).
4. For which customers are your services most *convenient?* Data shows that in the current market, convenience often trumps the lowest price. Building a warm, personable community space for local customers is also relevant to our next question…
5. For which customers can you create an intangible value add by offering a warm, supportive community experience? This may be customers who share some unique interest, life experience,

> or cultural background with you, or it may be those who are part of your local neighborhood. Or, if you're Boxed.com, it may be *all* customers if you build your systems right.

Of note, it may sometimes make sense for a sufficiently large company to run ad campaigns targeted toward multiple communities and demographic groups at once. McDonald's, for example, has engaged in marketing campaigns targeted to offer a sense of community to people of different backgrounds and cultures.

However, as a general rule it's a good idea to invest in only the *one or two most profitable* customer types you identify, and to master one target audience ad campaign with proven high ROI before trying to initiate multiple ad campaigns targeted toward different demographics.

Learning who your most profitable customers are will be key to optimizing your profit margins and your return on investment for advertising campaigns. But there are two more types of questions you'll want to consider before you actually build your campaign.

YOU KNOW YOUR CUSTOMERS—OR DO YOU?

Traditionally, when we talk about "customer demographics," we think of things like age, gender, ethnicity, income bracket, etc.. But the twenty-first century has changed this calculation in two important ways. While these stats may still be very useful to collect, they may not be your most powerful predictor of who will be a great customer. In the age of digital data collection, you can easily dig deeper to find out what your best customers *really* have in common beyond superficial characteristics.

In recent decades, many age, gender, ethnicity, income, etc. barriers have been broken down. Buyers of all sorts of industries and services are now more demographically diverse than they used to be.

Fortunately, advances in data collection and ad targeting also allow us to access information about our customers that may prove even more powerful. With most digital marketing campaigns, it is now possible to know things that tell you much more about customers, such as:

- Their daily hobbies and activities. "Tabletop gamers," for example, is now a demographic with a strong sense of community and very specific marketing sensibilities, both of which allow advertisers who target tabletop gamers to connect more powerfully than age, gender, or race-based assumptions might.
- Their interests, events they like to attend, and topics they like to learn about. Showing this kind of personalized interest can allow advertisers to draw customers in through offers or discussions that may, at first glance, not appear directly related to their product. These outreaches show customers that the advertiser is more than just a product: the company is a community member who understands what's important to the customer and wants to help.
- Any community or subculture they may belong to, including those that certainly don't show up on traditional demographic surveys. Communities and subcultures can sometimes be defined and targeted very precisely by studying the habits of your most profitable customers.

My own client, John DiJulius of The DiJulius Group, advocates the use of a set of questions he calls "FORD" to build excellent customer relationships. You'll recognize some of the FORD questions from the story of Boxed.com, where Boxed was able to almost completely automate methods for collecting these very important pieces of information and incorporating them into future customer interactions.

FORD stands for:

- Family. Who are your customers' loved ones, including pets? Is there a way to include gifts for them in your future interactions with the customer?
- Occupation. What does your customer do for a living? Is

there a way you can show that you know and support their profession?
- Recreation. What does your customer do for fun? Does your target audience have common shared hobbies that might serve as a basis for company promotions or community events?
- Dreams. Who do your customers *want* to be? How can you help support them in reaching these goals?

Knowing this information about your consumers, and even your staff, creates a clear sense of care between your company and your individual, which might make the difference between your customer choosing you or someone else.[1]

We'll see how the answers to these questions directly helped us to construct a powerful marketing promotion for Dr. Daniels in Chapter 3.

WHAT IS THE BEST CHANNEL TO USE?

One of the things that can make digital marketing feel so intimidating is the fact that the very *platforms* you can use to reach customers are often so specific and so rapidly changing. Different demographics consume media through different services, and each service may have its own algorithm for deciding who and how to show ads. That's why, when collecting demographic data, you want to *include* questions like:

- What search terms do your most profitable customers use most? Are there any terms that tie them together, no matter how unrelated to your product those terms may seem?
- What social media platforms do my most profitable customers use most?
- What streaming services or television channels do they watch?
- Do they use ad-blocking software? If so, which ones?
- Which influencers or other creators do they follow who may be persuaded to advertise your product?

- What does a typical day look like for your customer?
- Where do you go to learn about a product or service?
- How do you prefer to interact with vendors?

You can see how that's all a little bit more complicated than designing and running a billboard ad. You can also see how this is less intuitive for most CEOs than simply "going with their gut" on what the best way to reach customers is.

What if your CEO has had great experiences with Facebook marketing himself, but all of your most profitable customers are using Instagram and TikTok instead? What if your CEO has been running television advertisements for decades, but it turns out your customers spend twice as much time watching YouTube or Netflix as cable TV?

The good news is, when this type of data analysis is done properly, it's also *much* more powerful than traditional ad targeting mechanisms. You can appeal to your customers at a deeply personal level and ensure that you're only paying to show the ad to those customers to whom it is specifically suited.

This is what allows small but tech-savvy outfits like Boxed.com and the once-startup Amazon to take off so rapidly, even in the face of competition from massive established global corporations.

What solution did we find for Dr. Daniels by looking at the data around his customer lifetime value and return on investment from advertising? Let's find out.

CHAPTER 3
FINDING YOUR IDEAL CUSTOMER

IT'S no secret that today's market is incredibly competitive. In a world where anyone can start a new business using the latest technology and outstrip yesterday's giants within a few years, the market is full of both promise and terror.

On one hand, you could be the next wild success story; on the other hand, you could be the next titan to fall in the blink of an eye to bright, young competition.

Much of this war is being waged on the digital stage. With consumers doing more shopping online and spending less time in stores with each passing year, in most industries, those who win at capturing consumers' attention through ad space, content, and brilliantly designed websites are the ones who make the sales.

How can you make sure that's you?

The good news is, there's a less terrifying way to think about the modern market. While news headlines make it easy to envision it as a winner-takes-all shark tank in which a single brand can dominate multiple industries, the reality for consumers and business owners is much more complex.

The reality is that the opportunities that make the market so competitive are still opportunities. Every piece of technology or market trend presents an opportunity to zero in on the customers who would rather buy from you than from anyone else.

Because the truth is, customers prefer doing business with brands that understand them. They want brands that share and embody their values, and that understand their lived experiences in intimate ways. They want brands that solve *their* specific problems—not just big-box brands who do a passable job of providing solutions that work for most people.

The brands that have flourished in recent years have done so by hyper-individualizing their offerings. Outfits like Amazon, Facebook, and Google have found success through algorithms that customize customers' experiences to be wildly different according to the customers' own life. This hyper-targeting has made them irresistible to consumers.

This is within your power, too.

But the other great secret of business marketing is this: you don't need to appeal to *every* customer to win. In fact, if you are a small or medium-sized business, trying to appeal to everyone will do you more harm than good. You'll be wasting resources on low-return activities and missing opportunities to grab the attention of the customers who are just perfect *for you*.

How do you figure out who those perfect customers are for you, the ones who will jump at your advertising and spend money without needing to be asked twice?

You start by figuring out what makes *you* different from the competition.

Let's return to my work with Dr. Daniel's dental practice. His practice offered great customer service but was struggling to bring new patients through the door in response to competition from many local dentists, some of whom were savvier at digital marketing than he was.

What questions did we ask to help this practice?

- Who is your ideal customer? Who is likely to spend the most, or bring you the most referrals, if you can really impress them?
- How can you impress them? How can you offer something

that helps them in a deeply personal and meaningful way, but doesn't break the bank for you?
- How can you do this in a way that *your competitors aren't already doing?* How can you make sure these ideal customers notice you and *not* them?

For this dental office, the answer to the first question was obvious. Twenty-something women who have or are about to have families are the ideal target audience for dental services.

This is because women usually end up handling most health care decisions for their families. In addition to their own exams, they'll often schedule exams for their husbands, kids, and pass along recommendations for dentists to other moms who are new to running a family or new to the area.

Younger women are less likely to already be very attached to an adult health care provider, and more likely to bring in family members and recommend new patients for decades to come. For a dentist, this can mean that really impressing a single new bride or new mom adds up to tens of thousands of dollars over the course of years.

How could we reach young women who were just starting out their adult lives and families? How could we provide them with a service that would be deeply and personally meaningful to them, and that wouldn't put us underwater with free promotions?

When we framed the question like that, several answers jumped to the fore. The best one was this: free cleanings, exams, and whitenings for local bridal parties.

In this dentist's local area, weddings were a time when brides and bridesmaids went all-out to look their best in the photographs of his once-in-a-lifetime occasion. Why not make it super easy for them?

By offering free professional services, my client offered enormous value to young women who may not have seen a dentist in years in the midst of hectic adult life. They offered professional-quality cleaning and whitening for the wedding photos—but the free exams were the real stroke of genius. Often taking just a few minutes of the dentists' time, these exams allowed the dentists to offer to solve problems the women may not even have known they had.

This gap between your teeth? We can fix that for you. These stains? We offer a long-term whitening program. And by the way, here's a cavity that will cause you a lot of trouble in the future—but not if you let us take care of it within the next six months.

The free services, advertised using intelligent digital marketing services that targeted local brides and bridesmaids, got new customers in the door. When all was said and done, our client was netting new customers—whose lifetime value could be conservatively estimated at thousands of dollars each—for $15 per person.

The only reason they were able to do this so efficiently was the *specificity* of their targeting. They figured out who would be easiest to sell to, and who was likely to yield the highest return on investment in years to come, and crafted ads to appeal specifically to those customers.

Now, what if other dentists in the area had caught on and started offering the same thing? What if you were a different dentist, and your neighbor was already monopolizing bridal parties in your area? How could you most efficiently compete?

Well, this is where we get into the meat of setting ourselves apart. Where two businesses are competing for the same general customer population, there's always a subpopulation that each business is *more* uniquely equipped to serve.

Customers are drawn to people who are members of their own communities. They're drawn to people who understand their unique experiences and problems. The joy of doing business with someone who really *gets* you, for many customers, will even override minor matters of inconvenience or uncertainty.

What's a second dentist competing for brides in the area to do?

I encourage you to take a few minutes to answer the following questions for your own business and yourself, right now.

For your convenience, I've also included these questions in the companion workbook which can be downloaded at MiliaMarketing.-com/Resources.

1. Who is my ideal customer? Who is likely to be most

lucrative, if I get them through the door and really impress them?

2. Is anyone else already specifically targeting this audience? If so, what sets me apart from the competition? Consider questions like:
3. Location. Do I serve or hail from a specific region, city, or neighborhood that the competition does not? How does my location or local background allow me to understand these customers and meet their needs in a unique way? Is there a community identity I can appeal to, or benefits to keeping business within the community, which may encourage customers to do business with me instead of the other guy?
4. Background. Do I come from a different cultural background than the competition? If so, how does that allow me to uniquely understand and serve customers who share that background? How can I uniquely bond with them, based on this background?
5. Ethics & values. Is there a set of ethics and values that's particularly important to you? Do you manifest it in your business model, such as in your labor practices, supply chain, production methods, or assistance to charity? Many customers will pay a little bit more for a service if they know it is positively impacting a problem that is important to them.
6. Just make sure that your cause or process is somewhat unique or is combined with another unique aspect from this list. Lots of people are trying to operate carbon neutral now, for example, but you can be the only one to work with a specific set of farmers, to go above and beyond in a specific way, or be the only locally owned business in your industry that operates in this way.
7. Specialty. Is there a particular thing I do much better than the competition? A single product, service, or solution that you do better than *anyone* else can serve to draw customers through your door (or to your website, as the case may be) to see "the

best _____ in the world / country / region." If you impress your customers with this offering, there's a good chance they will also stay and come back to you for other needs in the future.

8. Age and generation. It's no secret that people of different ages see the world a bit differently. If nobody in your industry is already advertising to a specific age group, you may develop special appeal for customers by providing nostalgic or avant garde experiences that embody the values of the 1960s, or the 2020s, according to your own age and cultural background.
9. Subculture. Not all cultural differences are the result of location, ethnicity, or age. If you're a steampunk and also a coffee roaster, you can probably increase your sales by becoming the only explicitly steampunk coffee roaster for miles around. If you're a goth and also own a bookstore, there's probably good money—and relatively affordable ad space—in advertising specifically as a goth bookstore.

As tempting as it can be to avoid alienating some audiences by keeping our advertising bland and generic, "bland and generic" is actually the *worst* thing we can do in the age of targeted marketing. In an era where our customers likely have hyper-personalized ads being piped to them 24/7, spending money on ad campaigns that appeal to "everyone"—and therefore no one in particular—is often the equivalent of throwing our money away.

Of course, if you're a big business, you may consider designing multiple campaigns around multiple lucrative target audiences, or multiple uniquenesses your company has within its ranks. If you're a small or medium-sized business, it's probably a good idea to spend your resources appealing properly to *one* target audience, and then use the same protocol to expand to new ones once you've got a stellar return on investment from your first campaign coming in sustainably.

For printable and interactive worksheet versions of all the questions we've asked in this chapter, visit MiliaMarketing.com / Resources. You may find it useful to have each member of your leadership team fill out this worksheet independently, or to work on them together as a team to make sure you aren't missing any big opportunities.

This is a great time to put together ideas, but don't spend your marketing budget yet! Before you do that, we'll want to make sure you have several other items in place.

In the chapters to come, we'll discuss things to put in place *before* you buy ad space, to ensure that each ad click yields your maximum possible return on investment from the start.

CHAPTER 4
WHO DOES YOUR CUSTOMER WANT TO BE?

IN CHAPTER 2, we discussed a few tips for determining who the most lucrative customers for your business will be. We talked about the benefit of targeting customers who may buy in bulk from you or generate huge lifetime customer value through referrals. Now, it's time to take this to the next level.

We won't just ask ourselves who your best customers *are*. We'll ask who they *want* to be.

Adidas. Nike. Lululemon. Spotify. These are a few brands who have made their mark, not just by selling products, but by selling a customer persona.

"Impossible is nothing." With this slogan, Adidas boldly proclaims that Adidas gear is for people who overcome impossible odds. "If you are determined to do the impossible, buy Adidas. We'll help you do it."

Nike has taken a rather simpler route with their famous slogan: "Just do it." "If you are a doer," that slogan says, "you belong with Nike. We are your people."

The younger companies, Lululemon and Spotify, have taken distinctly twenty-first century approaches to cultivating a sense of identity for customers within their brand.

Lululemon's reputation and brand recognition relies heavily on thousands of "brand ambassadors"—community yoga teachers and influencers who are known and trusted within local fitness circles, and who profess to these communities that Lululemon is a company that shares their values. Lululemon states that it seeks out a particular type of "hard worker" to serve as its brand ambassadors, to remain consistent with the company's image as a brand for active, ambitious people who want to stay fit and practice self-care.

"If you buy our product," these influencers say, by their very public existence in Lululemon products, "this is the kind of person you'll be. This the kind of person you will become."

Spotify has taken the idea of the customer persona and the customer community to a much more granular level. Upon discovering that their customers responded with wild enthusiasm to any tools which allowed them to share their musical preferences and profiles—and thereby their personality and experience—with the world, Spotify seized on its ability to analyze customer data to create some deeply relatable, oddly specific customer personas and share them with the world.

"Dear person who played 'Sorry' 42 times on Valentine's Day," one iconic Spotify billboard read, "what did you do?" The image projected of a customer wasn't exactly inspirational, but it was funny and deeply relatable. The idea that customers could use Spotify playlists to express their deeply intimate emotions came across.

Many of the most successful brands, like those listed above, have realized that they are selling more than just a product. They are selling a set of *values*, which the right customers will choose to identify with and support.

What are the *values* of your business? Not just your selling point, but your personality? What kind of community are you inviting your potential customers to join?

For me, my target audience is strategists. They are key decision-makers who know the wisdom of investing in essentials. They are decision-makers who always want to act strategically, and who would rather build the best team of experts than do everything themselves.

They are, in short, wise people. And that's what was on my mind as I perused the gift shop of the South African cheetah reserve, wondering what to get my clients.

Gifting is a well-known method for strengthening customer-company bonds. When done poorly, it can come across as unsavory; I've seen people who, through a misunderstanding of their clients or their industry, seemed to think that merely showering people with expensive gifts would buy their business. That is not what makes gift-giving work, however. It's not about an exchange of value; as with gifting in any other context, it's about thoughtfulness and meaning.

This is a principle discussed in John Ruhlin's book *Giftology*. It's not the dollar amount of the gift's cost that makes a gift effective; it's what that gift says about your relationship with, and knowledge of, your client.

Buying someone a gift *at all* says that you're thinking of them, even when they're not around. Buying someone a gift that has deep personal meaning for your relationship, or which is precisely tailored to their tastes, says that they mean something to you. Enough for you to put thoughtful effort into selecting a gift that's perfect for them, or to think of them immediately when you see something they enjoy. This is the principle underlying gift-giving which successfully strengthens relationships between any two people, and it was the principle at play as I browsed gift shops in South Africa.

My clients deserved a little something from me. What was something that would speak to the nature of our relationship?

What first drew my eye was a set of elaborately carved coasters. The thick slabs of material were almost black in color, and so shiny that I initially mistook them for stone. Upon touching one, I found it to have the pleasant warmth and lightness of wood. The coasters had been carved into intricate three-dimensional frescoes artistically portraying the spirit of the "Big 5" animals of African wildlife: lions, leopards, elephants, rhinoceros, and buffalo. These gorgeous objects were unmissable, and completely unique. They were also perfect for one of my clients.

I thought of this client as soon as I saw the coasters. They were a distiller of fine spirits who prized artisan handcrafting in their own products, and I vividly remembered sitting down to sample their product on my first visit to their offices. Nothing I could give them would complement and strengthen their product better than a set of coasters as distinctive as their product and crafted with the same loving attention to detail. Every one of their liquors had a story, and these coasters were the same way. I had to buy them. I'd deliver them to my client to use in their offices at my next visit.

But many of my clients didn't have businesses which could so obviously benefit from the wares at this gift shop. What could I get *them*?

When my eyes fell on a smooth-polished stone statue, my face lit up. I'd found it! This statue, the shopkeeper informed me, was called a "wise man." It was crafted by local peoples to represent the virtues of wisdom, patience, and strategy.

That stone wise man now sits on the desk of John DiJulius, owner of The DiJulius Group. It symbolizes our shared values, and our commitment to grow together as experts in complementary industries.

Several of the brands I'll discuss in this book make use of gift-giving on a wider scale. They may include fields in their CRM for customer service agents to take relevant notes about the client's life and their states, allocating a budget to providing small gifts based on these details. Certain life events that clients mention such as birthdays, graduations, or bereavements may trigger the authorization of a gift sent to comfort or congratulate. Representatives may even be trained to collect information that can be used to personalize any gifts to reflect the customer's favorite things, their alma mater, or some specific attribute of the person being celebrated. This is just one example of a scalable gift-giving that builds relationships by acknowledging your company's meaningful role as a supportive companion on the customer's life journey.

Now, I've mentioned several times that personalization is important. All the gifting budgets in the world may fall flat, or even feel unsavory, if the company shows blatant misunderstanding of the customer's true wants and needs. Nothing screams "we want your money!" like a "gift" or "favor" that leaves the customer wondering, *Why on Earth would they think that I would want this?*

How can you know what your customers want, when people and their life journeys are so complicated? You can put in place plenty of mechanisms to collect data about customers and have customer service agents inquire about their needs, but sometimes you need to already know what to look for in order to even set up the optimal information-gathering measures.

How can you get to know your customer better? Many major brands have a highly developed way of doing just that, using the power of buyer personas.

THE POWER OF A BUYER PERSONA

Buyer personas combine the power of hard data with the power of human intuition to determine what customers want. These personas, or "avatars," are built using hard data skeletons gleaned from your market research, then fleshed out with human emotions to help you gain an intimate understanding of who your best customers are.

Buyer personas are constructed as much like real people as possible. They're assigned characteristics like age, experience level, educational resumes, job titles, and more attributes when appropriate. The goal is to really get inside the head of a person with these characteristics, which you believe are similar to the characteristics of your ideal customer.

Buyer personas or avatars may include filling in the blanks on all of the following attributes for your hypothetical buyer:

- Industry of work. Can include domestic labor, hobbies, and other types of unpaid work.
- Job responsibilities. What does this person need to get done in their life in order to succeed?
- Metrics for success. What does success look like for this person, in terms of measurable quantities?
- Values and abstract goals. How does this person want to be thought of by their peers? What emotions do they want to experience in life?
- Boss or supervisor. Who decides whether this person has succeeded?
- Trusted resources. Who is this person most likely to listen to?

- Barriers and concerns. What worries might cause this person to decide *not* to buy your product?
- Other important variables that determine what your potential customer is looking for in their life, and how they like to think of themselves.

A given brand may have several different buyer personas representing different types of people who are likely to spend money on their product. This is a good idea because it's important that a buyer persona be *specific*. If you are trying to understand different types of customers at once, you are less likely to be able to accurately understand any individual customer.

And it *is* individual customers who you are learning about in this exercise. Because all sales are, ultimately, made to individuals. All sales are made after these individuals have taken their life experience, material and emotional goals, anxieties and concerns, mental state, and more into account as they interact with your brand.

You stand the best chance of reaching customers if *you* can do this, too. If you can understand where these specific customers are coming from when crafting your marketing and your customer experience, you are more likely to be able to surprise and delight, and less likely to offend or simply fail to generate interest.

To get a better idea of how buyer personas look, let's make a few together. If you wish, you can download a buyer persona template from www.MiliaMarketing.com/Resources. You can use it to follow along here, or to profile your own top three most lucrative customer types.

ADIDAS BUYER PERSONA

Industry of work: Athletics. Adidas's most lucrative customers will be those for whom athletic performance is a high priority. This will include professional athletes and people for whom athletic performance is a major part of social status and personal achievement.

Job responsibilities. What does this person need to get done in their life in order to succeed? This may vary by product, with equipment designed for different sports appealing to different sub-audiences. What buyers will look for, then, is not "the best running shoe" or "the best basketball shoe," but "the company that knows sports inside and out and demonstrates knowledge of the different needs of different athletic tasks."

Metrics for success. What does success look like for this person, in terms of measurable quantities? Speed, strength, endurance, grit, concentration, and agility are all attributes that serious athletes will respond to when portrayed in a marketing campaign.

- Values and abstract goals. How does this person want to be thought of by their peers? What emotions do they want to experience in life? For serious athletes, athletic performance is the metric by which personal achievement, determination, and hard work are measured. Athletic performance is seen to reflect not only physical, but emotional and mental performance. As such, athletes will have the goal of achieving the impossible, both mentally, physically, and emotionally.
- Boss or supervisor. Who decides whether this person has succeeded? Serious athletes typically perform for personal satisfaction. Their most important judge of success is themselves.
- Trusted resources. Who is this person most likely to listen to? Athletes who are record breakers are seen as authorities in both the mental and physical aspects of their sports. At the local level, the athletes' own coaches and teammates are likely to be regarded as reliable sources of information about their sport.
- Barriers and concerns. What worries might cause this person to decide *not* to buy your product? Chief concerns might include whether your product is truly optimized for athletic performance, and whether its materials will hold up under extreme performance conditions. It may be beneficial to offer in-store test runs for athletes to sample your wares

themselves as well as, of course, obtaining endorsements from trusted experts in the field.
- Other important variables that determine what your potential customer is looking for in their life, and how they like to think of themselves. The most lucrative athlete-customers start early in life and may have to retire from their sport by middle age. As a result, targeting younger audiences will be important.

Given that buyer persona, how do you quickly communicate that you understand these values and are equipped with the expertise and materials to support them?

You do exactly what Adidas did. "Impossible is nothing," backed up by celebrity endorsements from top athletes.

LULULEMON BUYER PERSONA

Lululemon has become somewhat internet famous in recent years after employees revealed details of their buyer personas to internet audiences. These can serve as instructive examples for exactly how specific a buyer persona can get. Known examples of Lululemon buyer personas include:

- "Ocean," 32-year-old professional single woman who makes $100,000 per year. Ocean is engaged, has her own condo, travels, and spends an hour and a half per day working out.

It's easy to see why Ocean appeals to ambitious young women: she has a pretty great life. And if buyers purchase Lululemon, the company's ads suggest, they can reach Ocean's goals for themselves.

- Ocean's boyfriend, Duke. He is 35, makes over $100,000 per year, and engages in rugged outdoor sports. He surfs in the summer and snowboards in the winter. He has served as the buyer persona for their menswear line.

Using these two highly specific buyer personas, let's take a moment to dissect how Lululemon would answer the following questions in its buyer persona.[1]

- Industry of work. It doesn't matter what Ocean and Duke do for work, as long as it pays well and doesn't interfere with their freedom to travel and work out. Lululemon doesn't try to solve career-specific problems for its customers, but it does need customers who have both money to spend and time to devote to exercise.
- Job responsibilities. What does this person need to get done in their life in order to succeed? Lululemon customers have to be sharp, focused, and fierce to maintain their status as high-performing moneymakers. With their buyer persona and the images they use in marketing, Lululemon crafts the image of a professional who uses their workout as a means to support personal power and mental clarity.
- Metrics for success. Lululemon customers likely measure their success in terms of professional and financial achievements, but also in terms of lifestyle. This means they want gear that advertises their career and financial success, but supports these goals instead of detracting from them. Appealing to an audience that desires status symbols allows a brand to charge higher prices; in fact, higher prices may actually be seen as a desirable indicator of quality.
- Values and abstract goals. How does this person want to be thought of by their peers? What emotions do they want to experience in life? This audience wants to balance relaxed serenity with fierce determination. They want to work hard and be acknowledged for it, but also have the freedom to go on adventures and engage in self-care. Lululemon's ads project this persona, incorporating focuses both on achievement and performance and relaxation and serenity in their advertising. They promote the idea that achievement and serenity mutually support each other.
- Boss or supervisor. Who decides whether this person has

succeeded? Ocean and Duke probably want to believe that they are the only judges of their own success; but if we're being honest, what other people think is important to them. They don't just want to *be* high achievers with personal freedom; they want to be *seen* having those things, too. And buying and using Lululemon gear is a way to do that.

- Trusted resources. Who is this person most likely to listen to? Self-actualizers like Ocean and Duke are more likely to listen to trusted teachers and mentors than mainstream celebrity figures. They work with their own instructors and coaches and take a skeptical eye toward mass media. Coaches and instructors who actually work with potential Lululemon customers, then, are the ideal brand ambassadors.
- Barriers and concerns. What worries might cause this person to decide *not* to buy your product? Ocean and Mountain want to know that their products will work reliably, so as not to interrupt their sensitive routines. Personal testimonials from their own instructors and coaches will help them ensure this gear will support their lifestyles.
- Other important variables that determine what your potential customer is looking for in their life, and how they like to think of themselves. Ocean and Mountain value success, and value looking successful. That means the images they will respond to will be images of high achievers and people who look like they'd be competent and fierce in the boardroom as well as in the yoga studio.

How do you act on the information above? Precisely the way Lululemon has: with an emphasis on optimization, a balance of emphases on self-care and performance, and a program designed to elicit endorsements from thousands of local influencers and teachers around the country instead of relying on a few big-name celebrities who may be perceived as out-of-touch by the target audience.

MILIA MARKETING BUYER PERSONA

- Industry of work. Strategic decision-makers in companies selling products and services. Customers may come from any industry, but all share the goal of improving sales and brand recognition. Most often, these companies have $2.5 million or more in revenue and at least 15 employees.
- Job responsibilities. What does this person need to get done in their life in order to succeed? Increasing sales is likely to be the top priority, with brand recognition and reputation as a close second. They need additional marketing support and expertise to either assist their in-house marketing specialist or completely steer the marketing ship for the company. They want to focus on what they know best: running their business. Not getting stuck in marketing meetings, learning Facebook Ads, or building sales funnels online.
- Metrics for success. What does success look like for this person, in terms of measurable quantities? Success can be measured in revenue, quantity of new customers acquired, website views, search engine rankings, ad conversion rates, and more.
- Values and abstract goals. How does this person want to be thought of by their peers? What emotions do they want to experience in life? These strategists want to bring success to their brand and their team. They want to feel the satisfaction of not only personal achievement, but of helping other people grow. They take pride in creating jobs and making customers' lives better. Driven by efficiency and effectiveness.
- Boss or supervisor. Who decides whether this person has succeeded? At the end of the day, the numbers decide. These decision-makers tend to be working in the C-suite, so it is the performance of their business that directly tells them if their decisions are paying off.
- Trusted resources. Who is this person most likely to listen to? Industry experts such as fellow business leaders and well-

known marketing experts are likely to be trusted. Social proofs such as testimonials and case studies will be vital, as these decision-makers want to see proof of consistent results before investing their own resources in a product or service.

- Barriers and concerns. What worries might cause this person to decide *not* to buy your product? The most common barrier may be skepticism as to whether digital marketing can work at all. Lack of success with past marketing approaches may be a common feature, as many have likely tried hiring in-house marketing teams before seeking an outside agency. Some may also be older companies who are relatively new to digital marketing. Hard metrics and thorough explanations of my methods will be necessary to demonstrate that superior results are within their reach.
- Other important variables that determine what your potential customer is looking for in their life, and how they like to think of themselves. These decision-makers may be of any age, gender, or other demographic group. But they likely all have one thing in common: decision-makers are usually benefactors. They have gotten to where they are by being team players and holding concern for their team in their mind. As such, emphasizing the potential of wise decisions to create win/win/win situations will show these customers that you share their goals and values.

Now that you know who your ideal customer is, how can you adjust your messaging to attract people like that—or people who *want* to be like that—to your brand?

In the chapter to come, we'll discuss another way to use your buyer persona to understand your customer's experience of interacting with your brand and industry.

CHAPTER 5
YOUR CUSTOMER JOURNEY MAP

IN THE LAST CHAPTER, we mapped out our buyer persona—the "ideal customer" who we most want to do business with, and who our clients most want to be. This buyer persona encapsulates not only the best interests of our company, but also the best interests of our clients as far as who we can help them become. In this chapter, we'll see more of how understanding our customers, using a new set of tools, can help us to help them.

How many business owners have you known who complained of poor return on investment in their marketing? They had a great product, all the bells and whistles you're supposed to have, a respectable advertising budget, and a strong desire to grow—but their return on investment for advertising was nil.

In these cases it's easy to point fingers. If you had a marketing agency or specialist who failed to obtain results, it's easy to feel cheated. In rare cases, I've even seen owners and CEO blame *customers* for "making the wrong buying decisions."

But here's the thing: as a CEO, owner, or specialist, *you are responsible for* your company or your area of expertise. You decide who's hired to work on it, you decide what projects and budgets are greenlit, or you decide what proposals go to the leadership.

That's a very good thing! Because anything you are responsible for, you can *control*. To quote the Sword of Damocles (and also Spiderman), "with great power comes great responsibility." The good news for us is that the opposite is also true. Most of us don't have superpowers dropped into our laps, but by taking on *more* responsibility for our outcomes, we take on more power in the form of knowledge.

It turns out there is a *lot* we can control about how customers respond to our brands. Far more than many people realize. We just need to take responsibility for learning the variables that determine how customers respond to us.

A few years back, I had the privilege of working with a company who was supplying really top-quality building materials for homes. They were also doing everything they'd been told they were supposed to do by their marketing experts. They rented billboards, had radio ads, and paid top dollar for a web design team.

There was just one problem: none of it was working.

Despite pouring thousands of dollars per month into marketing, their showrooms had virtually no foot traffic. Their website leads turned out to be mostly spam. No one was beating a path to their door to hand them massive contracts.

Their in-house web team was baffled. On paper, they had all the boxes ticked. Everyone in a hundred-mile radius had to know their company. You could contact them right online.

So why wasn't anyone showing up?

THE HARDEST THING ABOUT DIGITAL

I mentioned that this company's marketing experts had done everything they were supposed to do—in theory. They'd checked all the boxes and had all the proper bells, whistles, and quantities. They *should* have had customers beating a path to their doors.

The problem is, major components of advertising are subjective. They aren't *just* a box you can check off on a page: they require a human understanding of the customers' experience.

This business had a website and ad campaigns that technically checked all the boxes, but they just weren't resonating with their customers.

This is the most important part of marketing. And, the hard truth is, there's no formula for getting it right every time. The best you can do is use tools like the ones provided in this book, and then use A/B testing to determine which approaches are actually working best.

In A/B testing, you simply test two versions of an ad, website, or product on test audiences. These are referred to as the "A" and "B" versions of the design, ad copy, or campaign. What's important here is that even tiny differences between the A and B designs may end up producing *massive* differences in your conversion and sale rates, and in your resulting revenue. In many cases, even marketing experts cannot tell you which version will bring in more money based on intuition alone. Actual on-the-ground testing is required to find out which ad will give you a higher ROI for the money you put into it.

A/B testing is the scientific method of marketing. It's the process whereby you test your hypothesis (your theory about how each ad campaign will go) and see once and for all whether things do play out that way in the real world. You do this with a small, limited budget *before* you decide which campaign to sink your entire advertising budget into. This increases the chances that you'll get the optimal return on investment for that advertising budget.

Even with A/B testing and analytics, you need to have a good idea of what customers are actually looking for in order to have highly effective ad campaigns to test. And that was where this business was falling flat.

The owner's-eye view of a business is very different from the customer's-eye view. We all know this intellectually, but actually behaving as though it is true is surprisingly difficult.

You know things about your product or service that your customer doesn't already know. Very often, you and your customer work in different day jobs, and you care about different things. If you work in an industry, it may be *decades* since you struggled to decide how to make a purchase in that industry, since you already know so much more about it than the average layperson.

Many marketers complain that industry experts are the *worst* critics and designers of advertising campaigns for that reason: their knowledge base is so totally different from the customers'. The ads that appeal to them are almost never the same ones that appeal to the people who need to buy their expertise.

Digital marketing will succeed if you do it right. But here's the hardest part about digital marketing: "doing it right" requires you to master objective analytics and deeply subjective questions. Questions like, "What is my ideal customer thinking?" and "How can I design an ad campaign that appeals to them, not to *me*?"

As an industry expert, how do you make sure the things you're saying are the things the customer needs to hear?

SEE THROUGH YOUR CUSTOMERS' EYES

Sue Stabe is the co-owner of Long and Short of It, a company which specializes in helping brands to understand the thoughts, feelings, and action patterns of their customers. I interviewed her about one of her favorite tools: the Customer Journey Map. Stabe's favorite tool expands upon a model developed by McKinsey & Company, adding additional "touch points" at which a brand had the opportunity to optimize their interactions with a customer. This map asks a series of questions that provide a systematic way of asking the right questions to determine how your potential customers experience your industry.[1]

"Understanding your customer is the foundation to all marketing and sales activities," Stabe told me. "You need to know what they are thinking, feeling, and doing within your category, as well as their perceptions of your brand. Many companies say they know their customer, when in reality they know a few demographics and an anecdotal comment or two. This isn't enough."

Indeed, anecdotes are infamously unreliable, and can drive massive losses for a business if that business proceeds assuming that a particular anecdote is representative of most customers' experiences. A business may not even realize this is happening; they may not be hemorrhaging cash, but they may have no idea that they *could* boost their growth tremendously using more rigorous data collection tools and customer journey mapping.

"A deeper understanding of their behavior and beliefs is needed to drive your messaging," Stabe continues. "You need to connect with them in a way that is meaningful and at a place that is relevant. There is so much content out there that you only have a short window to entice them to want to learn more."

For my own model, I add a stage that investigates the customer's daily life *before* they realize they have a need for your product, which helps you understand how to reach their awareness in their daily life, and a stage after a customer's first interaction with you, which addresses the question of winning their long-term, habitual loyalty. The end result looks like this:

1. Pre-trigger. For your most profitable customer, what is their ordinary life like? What experiences, passions, worries, and desires do they probably experience before they become aware of your brand? These are some of the same questions we asked in Chapter 1 when examining who your ideal customer is, and whether there is a subset of these customers who you are more well-equipped to understand than any other company.
2. Examining this stage, you can ask yourself questions like, "Where does my customer go on a daily or weekly basis, in-person or online?" "What do they think about and research on a daily basis?" "What kinds of entertainment do they consume?" This gives you good avenues to start thinking about how to precisely target these customers with your marketing.
3. Customer becomes aware of a problem or need that they must solve. This can range from an acute, pressing need like a health problem or car breakdown to a moment of aesthetic appreciation where a customer sees something and thinks, *I must have that!*
4. Useful questions to ask about this stage to improve your marketing include "If the customer wants to purchase my product, what problem are they trying to solve? and "What does the customer most want to hear when they realize they have this need?"
5. Customer explores different brands and products that

promise to meet that need. To add your brand to the list, the customer must be able to find you through your marketing interfaces.

6. Useful questions to ask about this stage include "How can customers find me?" "How are my most ideal customers likely to look for a service like mine?" and "How can I improve my rankings in their search engine results, ad placement, and placement on review sites?"
7. Active evaluation. The customer evaluates different options available to them, adding or eliminating businesses from their "might buy from" list as they go. They're likely to consider factors including price, convenience, their impression of the business's trustworthiness, and the precision with which a product meets their specific needs.
8. Questions to ask here can include, "Is price or convenience more important to my customers?" "How can I build trust with certified reviews and testimonials?" and "What other information and Frequently Asked Questions can I provide to show my ideal customers why my solution is best for them?"
9. After a period of evaluation, the customer chooses a business to purchase from. The biggest marketing hurdle has now been completed. If you can convince your customer to purchase from you once or twice more after this, there is a good chance they will form a habit of buying from you.
10. If your business was chosen by the customer, congratulations! If it wasn't, what can you deduce about *why* it wasn't based on your data and your customer journey map? Was your product not visible enough to the customer through their search methods? Was it not convenient enough to purchase or acquire? Or were you, perhaps, targeting the wrong customer all along on this journey; is there another group who might have preferred your client over the competition?
11. Sharing. After the customer has sampled your product, there is a chance they will tell their friends and family something

about the experience. This is a huge opportunity for growth for your business, as we discussed when we spoke about referrals under customer lifetime value.

12. How can you incentivize the customer to share a great experience and encourage others to do business with you? Might coupons for their friends and family's first visit be a useful way of tempting more customers to try your product? Can you supply them with something cute or delicious with the request that they share it on social media along with your brand name? Can you make it super-convenient for them to write a review on Google Maps?
13. Loyalty. If a customer has sufficient reason to buy from you again, each repeated interaction increases the chance of their *continuing* to buy from you for years to come.
14. So how can you increase the chance that they will want to buy from you a second time? Is there a coupon you could use that would give them great ROI? A loyalty card or app which would reward repeat purchases? Targeted sales emails optimized to appeal to this specific customer based on their previous purchase?

You can see how the customer journey map provides a systematic way of asking the right questions to determine how your potential customers experience your industry.

At some level, the fact that all customers pass through these five stages might seem obvious. But Stabe's Customer Journey model takes this research a step further. At each stage, she recommends asking specific questions about how the customer is feeling, thinking, and acting. Stabe's maps even allow businesses to identify "leaks"—points in the customer's decision-making process where your brand may be losing them due to a failure to understand or appeal to their experience.

"The customer decision journey is the key to mapping out the path to purchase for each target audience and category." Stabe describes creating multiple customer journey maps for multiple types of customers.

In one example, she chooses three types of clients to map separately: those with an acute need for the product and service that arose recently, those looking for long-term service providers in an urgent capacity, and those looking for long-term service providers in a non-urgent way. Each of these groups will have different feelings, thoughts, and take different actions along their customer journey.

Importantly, Stabe says, businesses cannot assume "once a customer, always a customer." Customers may defect to another brand for future purchases, even if they buy from you once.

"The actions and thoughts in the post-decision phase directly impact whether or not the brand will be in the consideration set during the pre-decision phase the next time they are in need for the product or service," Stabe explains. "The decision process is really a loop rather than a straight line.

"Each phase contains a couple of stages, to ensure the details are captured. Within each stage, we seek to understand what the target audience is feeling, thinking and doing, as well as the touchpoints they are using. After that, the pivotal points and moments that matter are determined. These are the most important points along the path to purchase. It's where you want your brand to be."

Anticipating a customer's feelings, thoughts, and touchpoints can seem like added work. But it is added work with tremendous reward. In the case of our example from earlier in this chapter, my client's marketing team had simply failed to understand the journey of customers who may be lucrative for their company. Customers were looking at their ads and website but seeing nothing that spoke to the feelings or thoughts they were having at that moment.

"Aligning sales and marketing tactics to the journey stages is incredibly powerful," Stabe explains. "They'll hit the target where they are when they are making that decision. It's the best way to get the most out of marketing spend."

Which might have been why my client, at the start of our work together, was getting essentially zero return on marketing investment.

What could this client's marketing team have done differently?

If you said "data and analytics" would help, you're right!

"Organizations collect the data for the journey in a variety of ways," Stabe explains. "And this data collection should be matched to your goals. We typically conduct a series of qualitative, individual, in-depth interviews to gather the insights.

"With a one-on-one discussion with a selection of your best customers or potential customers, you can go deep to really explore the emotion behind the behavior. When possible, this should be married with quantitative data about the target audience."

This is an excellent example of an opportunity to marry human instinct with data analytics. Data analytics are necessary to ensure that the customers you interview are similar to the majority of past and potential customers who will be good for your business. But when it comes to really understanding what these customers are telling you, it's human empathy and intuition that feed the creative process and turn those conversations into great marketing.

"Brands fall short when they don't socialize the journey internally," Stabe told me. "You want everyone to be speaking the same language. In a large company, the customer's journey impacts many departments, and the entire team can benefit from using the journey to align their efforts."

DIGITAL MARKETING GONE RIGHT

In the case of my own client who suffered from lack of resonance with their audience, we were able to turn their story around. We cut their spending on less-than-optimal advertising methods, upgrading their website to a more appealing—but not more expensive—design, which engaged customers by asking them the right questions from the very first click.

Perhaps most importantly, we revisited their advertising keywords, targeting, and their customer journey. It turned out that for this customer, their online advertising had been targeting the wrong people. While their choices of keywords and targeting had seemed logical to their previous marketing agency, they were not successfully targeting builders. This was a huge problem because home building companies, not individual customers, were the demographic most likely to make large purchases from this company.

By conducting additional research into who their most lucrative customers were, and how that audience behaved online, we were able to begin an SEO and ad targeting optimization campaign that ensured their content would be put in front of the people who were most likely to be hungry to purchase their product in bulk right away.

We made sure that the ads were reaching customers who would actually spend money with this business—and that the ads were successfully appealing to the feelings and thoughts of those who were looking to buy. We identified quick wins and opportunities to improve their SEO and created a long-term plan to dominate their online market. We collaborated and sat down with the client while reviewing past marketing reports, audited their marketing platforms, and identified the difference between a BAD lead (an unqualified customer) and a GOOD lead (a qualified customer).

Within 30 days of these changes, phone calls received as a result of their online advertising had grown by 40%. Even better, more of these customers were actually interested in buying their product and were well-positioned to do so. Fewer confused homeowners were calling, not quite understanding what the company offered, and almost all of the new leads came from companies who were knowledgeable about the industry and interested in buying large quantities of building materials.

We continued to optimize the company's ads and online presence, taking what our data showed was working best and optimizing that. After 60 days, we had increased their ad conversion rate by a factor of *fifteen,* from just 1.4% of viewers taking action to visit the company website previously to *23%* of ad viewers doing so with the new ad campaign. At the same time, we were able to *lower* the cost per engagement they were paying for their ad space by 14.4%.

We also optimized the website itself to form an immediate relationship with the customers who clicked ads. By adding interactive features such as an automated question-and-answer messenger program, we helped the customers to *feel* like they had a relationship with the company and like they'd already talked to us about their project as soon as they chose to engage with the chatbot. We added images and videos to show off the beauty of the products and the friendly, knowledgeable staff and owners. We added FAQs to address common customer concerns and answer customer questions about their projects right there on the website. This all helped to drive that 40% increase in phone traffic.

And remember: the customer journey doesn't stop with the customer clicking on your ad or picking up the phone to call you. Instead, successful use of the customer journey map covers a customer's *entire* experience.

While working with this company, we also identified another point where they were losing revenue needlessly. Our analytics showed that even when customers did reach out to the company from their website, the company staff was often not taking action to respond! Calls were going unanswered, voicemails and emails were not being received in a timely fashion, and their email automation to build relationships with customers who sent them form submissions was practically nonexistent. Tracking "lost revenue" quickly became a key metric that we used to show the client what these missed opportunities were worth.

This was especially troubling because this company had an average lifetime value of $5,000 in revenue per new customer. It would not have been unrealistic to project that tens of thousands of dollars were being lost each week by failure to answer phones, return phone calls, and otherwise support customers in making the decision to buy.

That may sound like a harsh assessment, but it's true of many businesses. And in a way, that's not surprising: your team specializes in the service you provide. *Not* necessarily in sales or marketing. That's exactly why bringing in a sales and marketing specialist with experience optimizing *every* step of the customer journey can help. Your team is busy serving your existing customers and managing your daily operations.

Without prompting and expert guidance, courting new customers can easily slip to the bottom of their to-do list. That's what had happened here. One missed call here, one forgotten voice message, one unanswered email inquiry there. None seemed urgent or essential to the company's daily operations, but all these missed opportunities added up.

Fortunately, our analytics showed us exactly where the problems were. They showed that answering the phone was more important than responding to emails, because people who called instead of emailing or using a form submission were more likely to follow through and buy.

This made perfect sense with a glance at the customer journey map: people who were facing an urgent deadline for an ongoing project were more likely to pick up the phone and call, whereas people who were merely curious about possibly, eventually buying were more likely to use form submissions. Where did we focus our limited energy, then? On responding to phone calls and using those calls to get customers to the showroom floor.

We were able to communicate exactly what was happening to the company's team members—we've got a whole chapter devoted to this vital component later in the book. Once they understood that each phone call or email received represented a potential $5,000 revenue boost, the executive team and floor workers alike moved those calls and emails way up on their priority list!

One particularly startling piece of math helped us make the case. Our aforementioned 40% increase in phone calls directed to the company by their new and improved ad campaign totaled 150 calls per month coming in from that campaign alone.

150 phone calls * $5,000 average customer lifetime value = $300,000!

Three-hundred thousand dollars per month. That's how much this company *could* have been making based on this one online ad campaign alone, if they'd aced every phone conversation and follow-up with a curious potential customer.

This is why it's so, so important to know who your best customers are, and to get inside their heads during the decision-making process. With proper targeting you can eliminate noise and competition, all while *saving* money on ad space thanks to your more focused, less general audience.

Business was so good that the company opted to keep working with us in the long-term.

When we first cut the billboard and radio spending, the company was spending less on advertising than they ever had before. But within a few months, their return on investment from the online spending was so good that they began to pour more money into online ads.

Since every dollar of advertising spend generated several dollars in ROI, there was no longer any limit to how much they could spend on digital advertising; now, the only limit was how many customers they could realistically serve. To complete your own customer journey map and help your team to get inside your customers' head, visit MiliaMarketing.com/Resources.

CHAPTER 6
HOW DO YOU KNOW IF YOUR MARKETING IS BAD?

"HOW IS your marketing performing for you?" That's one of the first questions I ask clients in our initial consultations. When people are coming to me for help, their answers are often less than enthusiastic. And with alarming frequency, the answer turns out to be "I don't know."

It can be easy to lose track of how well your marketing is working for many reasons. With traditional media like billboards, TV, and radio, it can be very difficult to know how many customers are taking action when they see your ad. While there are ways to do this, such as giving out different phone numbers in different ads and seeing which numbers receive more calls, you can't get the same level of detail about precisely who is responding to your ads, and what might be stopping them from buying, as you can in digital media.

This is one reason I chose digital marketing as my area of expertise: I feel it allows me to offer customers the greatest value and the greatest optimization. I *always* track *everything,* and I advise my clients to do the same. Every single data point you collect about who is interacting with your marketing in what ways is data you can use to optimize your marketing to get better results in the future.

Tracking these metrics is the *only* way you can know with certainty how well your marketing is working for you. If you can't track customer responses to your ads, you're left to make uninformed guesses when figuring out how you can improve.

The data you collect can yield very surprising insights as to how you can increase your sales and grow your customer base. Let's look at a case study where the result of collecting hard data on customer interactions was almost the *opposite* of what my client's head of marketing expected, and the changes we made with this data transformed the client's business.

SO MUCH POTENTIAL, SO LITTLE GROWTH

When I met Dr. Kim of Cornerstone Foot Care, she and her husband, Mark, were puzzled. Dr. Kim knew she provided excellent services: her customers raved about her online. Mark was her marketing coordinator, and he'd been running a direct mailing campaign to try to bring customers through the door.

The couple had worked hard to build this business. Dr. Kim was known to spend long hours ensuring that patients had everything they needed. She did her best to build an atmosphere of care and compassion that patients would feel comfortable walking into. Mark had worked just as hard, putting long hours into trying to figure out the best ways to communicate the business's values to potential customers.

And yet, new patients *weren't* walking through the doors. The patients Dr. Kim had were mostly long-timers, with few new faces to be found. And for many hours each week, the clinic stood empty.

Dr. Kim and Mark knew it was time for Cornerstone Foot Care to grow. But how could they make that happen, when no form of advertising they tried seemed to work?

First, Dr. Kim and Mark looked at industry-specific advertising solutions for podiatrists. These were shockingly affordable—sometimes suspiciously so. Not satisfied that marketing teams who offered almost frighteningly low rates had the experience and motivation they needed, Dr. Kim and Mark kept searching.

When they came to me, the first thing I proposed was A/B testing.

We would test many different ad designs and marketing approaches, and measure empirically which ones performed best when it came to *actually* bringing new patients into the clinic. Dr. Kim and Mark liked that idea.

To design these pages, I asked myself: what if I were a patient with a foot problem?

Foot problems can be embarrassing and awkward. They can also be painful and urgent. If I had a medical problem with my foot, I wouldn't want to tell someone that by giving them my contact information and then waiting to hear back. I wouldn't want to sign up for a newsletter which would send me updates at some point in the uncertain future. I would want to call to get all my questions answered *now*, preferably in a way that left no paper trail until after I'd decided that I actually liked and trusted the provider. If I liked what I heard on the phone, I might book an appointment on the spot.

One of the things we tested in our early work was this: which performed better at actually getting new customers into the clinic? A contact information collection form, or a phone number customers could call immediately to ask questions and potentially make an appointment?

Mark was skeptical of digital marketing. He didn't think it was likely that people would make their healthcare decisions thanks to online advertisements or newsletters. He feared that, jumping into the hypercompetitive digital fray, we may end up throwing away money without bringing in leads.

Mark was also skeptical about whether customers would want to take time out of their busy schedules to actually dial a phone number, instead of accessing information online. In his mind, making a phone call was more work than filling out an online form. In many circumstances, that might have been true; a phone call might have been a higher barrier to entry. But for customers looking to treat acute medical problems, I suspected that a contact method which gave them real-time feedback would feel more satisfying.

Which of us was right? There was no way to say until *after* we'd tested both approaches.

Here's why A/B testing is so powerful: the option that *seems* intuitively correct is often not actually the one that is most effective at convincing customers to take action. The only way to ensure that your marketing method is the best one available to you is to test it against *other* marketing methods in small, controlled experiments, and see which actually produces more results.

When we ran the ads with the phone number, Dr. Kim's phone started ringing off the hook. The tracking features I'd made sure we built into our ad campaigns made it clear that this approach was bringing in more than twice as many customers per advertising dollar as the form submission approach.

And this wasn't the end of the story. Once the phone was ringing, there were many more opportunities to use data-based optimization to turn those phone calls into patient visits. What we did with Dr. Kim's call tracking is an excellent example of the drastically underutilized power of data.

WITHOUT CALL TRACKING, YOUR BUSINESS IS FLYING BLIND

I love call tracking because it helps with marketing ROI so much. Call tracking is neglected by many businesses to their great loss; when used properly, call tracking is an easy spot to optimize factors like the strength of your business's relationship with its customers, the percentage of calls you're missing from potential customers, and more. I set up this service for all of my clients, and I'm including details about the platform I use so that you can to the same on your own.

For most of my clients, phone calls are a big component of the marketing funnel. Calls are one of the main ways to either bring in new leads or convert an existing lead into a customer. Without the platform I use, called CallRail, we'd be very limited in judging the performance of the campaigns we're running.

Ever wonder why often, when you call a business, you get an automated message that says, "This call may be recorded or monitored"? Here's why that happens: platforms like CallRail allow businesses to track the subjects that current and potential customers are calling about, identify patterns or problems that appear across multiple calls, and more.[1] Countless businesses have seen how call recording alone has made a serious impact on their bottom line by improving the customer experience and their relationship with the brand.

I've had clients who think they don't need call tracking because they think they don't get many phone calls. Every single time, without exception, they've discovered that they were getting a lot more calls than they'd realized. They simply weren't giving these calls the full credit they deserved as far as their potential benefits to their business; as a result, potential business was being lost.

As Dr. Kim's phone started ringing off the hook, challenges that will be familiar to any business owner arose.

Some calls were coming in after business hours, and it was hard to make time to answer those in a reliable and timely fashion. Even during business hours, staff weren't always able to get to the phone and answer all the calls immediately. People were sometimes put on hold. When the phone was picked up, hurried staff might try to answer the potential customer's question and move onto the next customer on hold as fast as possible. That was not the best way to convert new customers.

Growth stages are always a happy problem. A business owner is ecstatic to see growth, but they may not immediately have the capacity to handle it all with grace. Fortunately, using best practices and call tracking, we could identify precisely the areas that needed improvement to get the best possible results for Dr. Kim's growth.

At first, Dr. Kim struggled with the same mindset challenges as many of my clients. She and Mark weren't used to placing so much importance on phone calls. They underestimated how many they were getting, and once they started getting more than they could handle, they were reluctant to increase staffing just for the purpose of handling phone calls.

But with the help of CallRail, we were able to prove to them that it was so, so worth it. And this proved to be instrumental in their business's massive growth in the coming months.

At first, Dr. Kim and Mark were shocked to simply see how many calls were being missed because staff weren't available to pick up the phone. That motivated them to look further into what they were losing in those missed calls, and how they could address the situation.

The importance of staffing every call cannot be overstated. You might only get one call from an interested client per month; but for a small business, that one call could be your best client of all time. If you don't have the infrastructure in place to track and respond to calls in a timely fashion, you might miss the opportunity that could have taken you to the next level.

And remember, this is coming from a digital marketing guy; I mostly prefer computers. But I still can't overstate the importance of call tracking and management to my clients' businesses.

For Dr. Kim's practice, we were able to assign an average call value to each conversion. In order to do that, we took the revenue brought in from calls so far and divided it by the number of calls. By doing this, we were able to show how much money (on average) each of those calls brought in. This allowed us to put a number on the value of missed calls, which allowed Kim and Mark to make more informed business decisions.

For example, if we came up with an estimated call value at $100 in revenue for each call we received, and we received 200 calls in one month, we could then claim $20,000 in potential revenue from a single month's calls. This enabled us to show the true ROI or Return on Ad Spend (ROAS) from our online campaigns which were bringing in those 200 calls per month.

We were also able to demonstrate the value of investing in hiring and training staff to optimize the value of each call. Through this math, Dr. Kim and Mark came to the decision to staff the phones at their clinic until 9 p.m. each day, and to train staff in best practices for converting phone calls into appointments. The result was enormous growth in Dr. Kim's customer base.

For Milia Marketing, using this approach with our clients not only improves our relationship with existing clients, but also strengthens our reputation and helps us earn new clients by proving the value and efficacy of our work. Potential clients can know exactly how much revenue they're making from their investment with us, and therefore know that it's worth their hard-earned money.

One of my favorite slogans in marketing is this: "If you can measure it, then you can improve it."

Call tracking for your business is essential, so that you can measure the success or failure of your marketing efforts through the abundance or lack of phone leads coming in. If you can make incremental improvements each week using the information that call tracking data provides, that positive cumulative effect over the long term will build on itself like compound interest and contribute hugely to your success.

Should your business use call tracking? Here are some important questions to consider:

ARE YOU SEEING THE WHOLE PICTURE OF YOUR LEADS?

Trying to determine what kind of experiences customers are having with your brand, and why they aren't buying, is not a fun experience when you're missing many crucial pieces of data.

Typically, web form fills are not enough to see what's happening in your business. Some people like to call you instead of filling out a web form. Exactly how many customers prefer to call vs. correspond online will depend on your industry, but anyone who needs a problem solved *now* or who has a major proposition for you is likely to prefer a phone call over a web form. You have to track who is calling you, and what they are saying, in order to find out what your business may be missing with less-than-optimal phone responses.

I once had a client who didn't want to spend money on call tracking for the first several months of our relationship. After persistently raising our concerns over the span of almost a year, they finally decided to install call tracking. After a few months, we discovered that for each web form fill they received, they had an additional three phone calls.

Before call tracking, if they had 100 web form fills, they thought that their cost of acquisition per lead was very high. After adding the monthly 300+ phone calls, they understood that they were getting many more leads for their investment than they'd realized and were happier with our marketing efforts. Now, they were able to invest more into their phone resources and capture more of those leads as lifelong customers. We weren't flying blind anymore.

ARE YOU MISSING OPPORTUNITIES?

Maybe your staff are saying that the phones have simply not been ringing. We had a situation where one of our franchise clients had 13 locations across Canada, and their franchisees were saying they weren't getting phone leads.

After we installed call tracking for a few months, we immediately found out that over 38% of the calls were not being answered during regular business hours each week! This client was missing 240+ phone calls each month. Is that a worthwhile piece of business intelligence for the business owner to have? We think so.

CAN YOU IMPROVE YOUR NEW CUSTOMER EXPERIENCE?

Sales and customer retention are the lifeblood of any business. With call tracking, every call can be recorded for quality assurance. You can check the call quality of your phone staff, sales team, and even call center. Send your team the call recordings in order to provide constructive feedback, training, or praise.

With call tracking, you can also measure under-appreciated variables like the amount of time a customer spends actually talking to your staff (not on hold!). In general, the longer a potential customer speaks to a sales representative, the more likely they are to actually buy the product. The longer an existing customer spends speaking to a staff person, the stronger their relationship to your brand is likely to become.

As a psychological effect, you'll probably have more happy customers getting proper service if your employees know every call is being recorded. Encouraging sales representatives to focus on cultivating quality of relationship, instead of quantity of calls, may also take the stress of rushing off and boost conversion rates as a result of stronger relationships and better customer experiences.

Imagine that your team's phone closing ratio is 10%, and they receive weekly training and feedback based on their recorded calls. If you could see an increase to a closing rate of 12%–15%, or a larger average sale size as a result of a stronger customer relationship, what would that do to your bottom line?

WHAT IS THE QUALITY OF YOUR PAID PHONE LEADS?

After learning your *full* lead count, you can spot check your recorded calls and determine the quality of the leads. Are the people calling in really potential customers? If you find that you get tons of non-lead calls, you can optimize your targeting to be more likely to target first-time customers with high purchasing potential. On the other hand, if your call leads are already giving you a huge ROI, you can invest more!

For Dr. Kim's practice, the proof was in the huge volume of phone calls the clinic was now receiving, and the flood of *new* patients coming through the door. Soon, even Mark agreed that it would be wise to put all of the clinic's advertising budget into this approach.

We kept looking at the tracking data to optimize our results. It turned out that a large portion of the calls were being missed when Dr. Kim and her receptionist clocked out at 5 p.m.: dozens of patients were calling to schedule appointments after business hours, when they themselves had gotten off of work. By keeping her office staffed until 9 p.m., Dr. Kim was able to capture almost all of the calls that came into the clinic—and sign up a large portion of the callers for new patient appointments.

In the end, Dr. Kim and Mark got the growth they always knew they could achieve. They are now training a small army of new receptionists to handle their volume of incoming calls, and have purchased a new, larger building to accommodate all their new patients. The new patients they'll be able to handle with more staff and more space will more than pay for themselves.

I am so proud to have been part of Dr. Kim and Mark's journey. They always had what it took when it came to their craft, their expertise, and their passion. But like so many amazing service providers, they struggled to let the world know what they could do. Their passion was expertise, not marketing. That's why they needed a partner whose passions included Google ads management, Google display retargeting conversion rate optimization, and call tracking.

CHAPTER 7
OPTIMIZE EVERY STEP

DR. KIM and Mark's story illustrates a principle that plays a huge role in the success or burnout of countless businesses: What constitutes "good marketing" can become a point of major disagreement in the boardroom.

As we noted in Chapter 1, some leaders will insist on sticking to their own intuition no matter what the data shows. Others may even believe that data collection itself is a waste of time and money, since they think they already know how to reach their customers. Just because you see another thought leader in your space create a campaign, post on social media a certain way, or have a certain email design, does NOT mean that it's going to automatically work for your business. Your businesses might have different strategies and target audiences, or their approach might not be working as well as you might assume.

This would be fine, if not for the fact that people who take this approach are often wrong. They often struggle to make the necessary sales to fuel their business. Some will even claim that the problem is not with their marketing, but with external realities such as "problems" with competition and demand which they have no control over. These businesses may end up feeling that the tide of the market has turned against them, and that it's so overpowering there's nothing they can do unless outside conditions change.

That's not a very empowering mindset. The truth is, it is possible for *any* business to survive and indeed thrive, no matter *what* the market does. All that is required is the following:

1. Know what the market is doing. What is your competition doing that customers are responding to? What do customers want? The answer is almost never *just* "lower prices"—there are countless value adds that customers will happily pay more for, and these are often non-physical. You just need to figure out what those are. What are their pain points?
2. How can you meet that demand using your business' existing assets? There is always a way. It may just require thinking outside the box.
3. How can you know if your marketing and products are *working* before spending huge amounts of capital on them?

You can probably guess what I'm going to say here. Data, data, data.

Marketing spending, like all spending in business, is about return on investment.

How much money in sales are you making for each dollar you spend on marketing? Have you tested different marketing approaches to see which one has the highest ROI? Have you analyzed your customer demographics to see which customers are the most lucrative to target, and what *they* respond to best?

If you don't *know* the answer to any of those questions, or if the answer to any of them is "no," your business is not performing as well as it could be. In fact, it's likely that you're leaving a significant amount of money on the table in your attempt to be frugal and efficient.

Answering these questions requires looking at specific numbers and data collection techniques. These are the techniques you need to know and *use* if you want to optimize your profits.

KNOW YOUR CURRENT MARKETING ROI

This may sound incredibly basic, yet many businesses neglect to do it. Some deem it too burdensome or expensive to closely monitor their overall ad conversion rates, never mind the conversion rates for specific ad campaigns.

Businesses that don't keep an eagle eye on their advertising ROI may feel that it would be inefficient or irresponsible to hire someone to do this work. But you know what's much *more* inefficient and irresponsible? Losing thousands to millions of dollars in sales monthly because you didn't spend an extra few thousand to analyze, test, and optimize your ads.

What *is* your ROI on each advertising dollar you spend? If your business runs multiple lines of ads, what is your ROI for each one? What does that tell you about where to invest in the future? Are there any advertising methods for which you have no way of *knowing* their ROI? If so, how can you build a method to collect that data into your future advertising campaigns? If you know the ROI for the various ad campaigns you're running right now, you can enter the data you have into the worksheet found in the companion workbook available at at MiliaMarketing.com/Resources.

Once you've crunched the numbers, it will become clear which types of campaigns might be best to pursue for future marketing directions.

As we mentioned in a previous chapter, the sheer *number* of customers or sales you bring through the door is not the whole story when it comes to optimizing your marketing ROI.

For businesses with a wide range of possible customer spend, certain customers may create orders of magnitude more revenue for the amount of effort your business puts in than others. If your business model allows it, some customers may spend $5 and never come back. Others will buy big-ticket items, buy in bulk, or become lifelong loyal patrons.

Who are the most profitable customers for your business? How do you figure that out? And how do you figure out how to bring in more of *those specific customers* for less marketing spend using your marketing campaigns? These are also variables that you can—and probably should—track, analyze, and optimize with the proper data collection tools in place.

Once you know the answer to those questions, your marketing transforms. You can learn how to use marketing budgets to reach loyal, lifelong customers instead of struggling for each individual sale.

To know how effective each marketing campaign you run is, you need to know a few other metrics. After all, making a sale is a multi-step process.

You must first:

1. Attract a customer's attention.
2. Successfully convert their attention into a visit to your website or store.
3. Successfully convert that visit into a sale.
4. Successfully convert that sale into a long-term relationship.

Each step of that process has the potential to succeed or fail, often at rates that differ wildly for different approaches. Tracking online conversions are important, but optimizing through to the finish line when the sale is closed and the customer relationship nurtured are also vital.

This is why it's important to have a CRM setup and marketing/sales team closely working together; while some business owners make the mistake of viewing these as separate domains, in reality it is impossible for one department to get great results if the other is not supporting them well.

To optimize your ROI, then, you need to know *which approaches work best* for your most lucrative customers at every step of the process.

These numbers are called...

CONVERSION RATES

A conversion rate is the rate at which one action is successfully converted into another action. Conversion rates to monitor include:

- The rate at which your ad appearing on someone's screen converts into them clicking on your ad.
- The rate at which a visit to your website results in an actual sale.
- The rate at which a phone call results in a sale.
- The rate at which a first sale results in repeat sales from a loyal, habitual customer.

For each step in the process I mentioned above, conversion rates can be measured and optimized. When you know where conversions aren't happening, you can take action to fix that problem. If you *don't* know where conversion rates are lacking, on the other hand, you may pour money into entirely the wrong step, only to lose customers at a later step in the process or never even get them far enough to benefit from your investment.

These types of rates can be tracked for physical advertising too, but this may require more effort and yield less precision. I only recommend the use of billboards for companies with bigger advertising budgets, for example, because it's almost impossible to effectively track what percentage of people who see your billboard actually become customers. With digital marketing approaches, on the other hand, clicks, purchases, and new customers can be tracked and optimized precisely.

For digital marketing, conversion rates are usually recorded in percentages. What percentage of customers who are shown your ad click on it?

Properly engineering your company website with data analytics, or building in other tracking methods (such as questions about how customers found your brand on your order form, or discount codes that are only revealed to customers who see specific ads) can make it easier for you to track how many actual sales are coming from specific marketing campaigns, from word of mouth, and from other venues.

Once a customer has made their first sale, be prepared to track their lifetime activity—including how they first came to know your brand. That's how you'll learn which marketing approaches are bringing in your most lucrative customers, and what your *real* return on investment for marketing campaigns is.

TEST BEFORE YOU INVEST

I've referenced this a few times so far, but I wanted to make one thing very clear: you'll get your best average return on investment if you test several marketing approaches with small budgets and excruciatingly test each one's effectiveness *before* you invest your whole budget into one ad.

This form of A-B testing—a form of test that directly compares which options customers prefer for ads, web design, products themselves, and more—gives you the chance to know with certainty which ads are going to give you the best ROI before investing your whole budget.

What if you test three ads and find that one yields double the clicks compared to the others? Would you have chosen that ad design out of intuition alone, or would you have chosen one that would get you half the ROI or less?

What if you find out that one ad yields far more lifelong customers while others fail to target these most lucrative relationships? You could cut your marketing budget drastically—or better, increase your revenue drastically by shifting to emphasis on this ad type.

Never underestimate the power of testing to conduct research and produce data. That data is your north star when it comes to marketing your products.

YES, YOU REALLY NEED TO KNOW

Some of you who are reading this may still be thinking that this sounds like a lot of work. If you're not already working with a digital marketing company, it may sound like you need to re-engineer everything about your advertising from the ground up in order to collect the necessary data to optimize your results.

Do that. Totally do it.

In the preceding chapters, we've discussed the sad fact that many cultural giants that were once seen as untouchable fell due to failure to adapt to the rapidly changing market. Even as life has gotten better than ever for consumers, who now enjoy hyper-targeted ads for precisely the products they will love and can usually get these products delivered right to their doorsteps within a few days, companies that fail to change their ways to take full advantage of improving technology find themselves bankrupt.

But there's a success story in here, too. The success of the scrappy startup that begins with few to no resources, but grows by orders of magnitude within a few years. They succeed because they design all of their systems from the bottom up to collect as much data as possible and use that data to design the most efficient possible processes.

Data collection and bottom-up design are what has allowed companies like Boxed.com to win a loyal market share, and to *afford* to make the kinds of investments that make customers love them in a hyper-competitive world.

The purpose of this Part I has been to give you an idea of how rapidly the world of digital marketing is changing, and how, by being proactive, you can use that to your advantage instead of experiencing it as a weakness.

In Part II, we'll talk more specifically about how to accomplish the three major components of gaining loyal customers:

1. Grabbing their attention. It's not enough just to stand out. You also have to offer a clear, compelling message that motivates customers to buy. We'll look at how to do that.
2. Giving them a great experience. Customers hate being inconvenienced. In a world of streamlined websites, users want to be able to find exactly what they're looking for in just a few clicks. How can you make your online experience as warm and convenient as possible?
3. Guiding them to buy. Your messaging will determine whether users really feel that your product or service will solve their problem. Use your messaging wisely.

4. Building loyalty. As we've covered here, a lifetime customer is the holy grail of marketing results. How can you make sure you build warm, personal relationships with customers in the most efficient way possible?

We'll discuss all this and more in the chapters to come.

PART TWO
STAND OUT

CHAPTER 8
THE ENORMOUS POWER OF TINY CHANGES

IN DECEMBER 2020, I received an email from the Czechoslovakian company Tlusty & Co. A purveyor of bespoke, high-quality leather goods, Tlusty & Co. was founded by a traditional Czech leatherworker in 1990 after the fall of communism. The company grew into a community of passionate people who loved to work leather with their hands.

Although the market for handmade leatherwork had shrunk as cheaper, mass factory-produced shoes and bags flooded the market, these artisans refused to give up on the craft that they loved. They were determined to preserve the traditional leather handcrafting technique that had been passed down from past centuries.

The founder of Tlusty & Co. knew they could make leather goods that were stronger, more beautiful, and ultimately more friendly to the environment and to workers' rights than the mass-produced alternatives. As a bonus, they could offer a high level of product customization to their customers since they would be creating each product entirely by hand.

The company survived the influx of mass-produced goods from around the world and the global financial recession following the COVID-19 pandemic, which hit their community particularly hard. Tlusty & Co. jumped into action, using their facility to recruit over 100 local seamstresses to sew cloth masks and protective face shields for their local community.[1] But still, profits dropped. Many people in their local community simply didn't have the money to spend on luxury goods at the time.

Now, one thing became clear: their competition had gone global. Tlusty & Co. needed to do the same thing.

I was privileged to be the recipient of their request for help entering the U.S. market. They had an amazing product, but little idea of how to reach U.S. audiences in the super-saturated American advertising sphere. Everyone in the world wanted to gain access to one of the largest and most lucrative target markets in the world. How could a small group of artisans from Europe stand out?

Easily, I told them. It was all about mastering data. No matter how big the advertising budget of their competition, we could still optimize Tlusty & Co.'s online presence and ads to precisely target the customers who would love their wares more than those of any competitor.

This would not be *simple*. It would involve optimizing dozens of variables. To give you a rough idea of the complexity of the task, this included:

- Analyzing keywords and putting together a massive keyword strategy.
- Mapping and implementing keywords to specific landing pages to build keyword relevance.
- Redirecting old product, category, and subcategory URLs to relevant pages.
- Cleaning up numerous technical issues and improving website speed.
- Restructuring the site navigation and architecture.
- Setting up popups to start collecting email addresses.
- Running A/B tests on popups to improve email subscriber conversion rate.
- Beginning to segment their list to better understand customers that purchased specific products for more relevant emails.

- Creating paid Facebook ads pointing to select blog content.
- Using influencer outreach and promotions through bloggers and Instagrammers for product placement and giveaways.
- Regularly pinning products on group boards and Tlusty's own board.
- Pushing promoted pins on top-performing blog content.
- U.S. competitive analysis
- Mapping out the competitive landscape.
- Qualifying competitors by their audience size and market potential.
- Revealing closest rivals online and research their digital strategies further.
- Analyzing competitor SEO efforts.
- Keyword gap analysis.
- Spying on their ad campaigns.
- Content marketing and PR competitive analysis.
- Creating U.S. buyer personas and audit and target audience analysis.

You get the idea. There *was* an intimidating amount of data to get through, and an intimidating amount of expertise required to optimize it all. But that was exactly the point. By ultra-optimizing all of this data, we could easily outperform the bigger brands in ROI per advertising dollar spent. We could find an advertising strategy that would turn Tlusty & Co.'s seeming weaknesses—their newness to the U.S. market, their small size and labor-intensive process—to their extreme advantage in the eyes of the right customers.

After all, anyone reading the story above can see that Tlusty & Co.'s work is valuable. But would that alone be enough to get thousands of customers to buy their products? If it could, every small business in the world would be thriving. Instead, to make mass sales and build a broad reputation, we needed to harness the power of data.

There will always be a human element to business. But now, it's time to bring our *other* superpower to bear. This is the power of data analytics.

In the case of Tlusty, we knew that sustainable SEO domination is a long-term game. But we also knew that Tlusty needed new customers *now*, and we worked to optimize their targeting and page views as much as we could within a few months of their campaign. Within a few months, we succeeded in procuring:

1. Altogether, a 94% increase in website visits (counting organic and paid visits), including a 77% increase in organic (unpaid) daily traffic, from an average of 381 up to 674 daily visitors.
2. A 182% increase in their Twitter impressions and a 58% increase in their Facebook page views.
3. An increase in their total monthly pageviews from 11,430 average visitors to 20,220 visits per month.

While Tlusty's entrance into the American and international markets is still in its early stages, the company has effectively doubled its presence in the minds of English-speaking customers at relatively low cost by using the care and expertise necessary to optimize its web design, its paid media targeting, and its SEO.

How can your company accomplish the same thing?

TAKE YOUR ANALYTICS TO THE NEXT LEVEL

If your company already has a marketing department, you're familiar with market research and data analytics. In market research, you look for cold, hard numbers about who's buying what. You may use surveys or focus groups to try to determine if there are customer needs and desires that aren't being met by existing products.

In this way, you can use data to project who is most likely to buy your product and what new products may make a big splash. In one famous example, chunky-style tomato sauce was invented after one food company's focus groups found that a large proportion of customers cited "chunkiness" as a characteristic of their favorite sauces, and no one in the industry was making or marketing a sauce specifically made to appeal to that desire.

Market research is important to get the broad strokes of product development and marketing right. But often the *real* cash cow lies in the much less glamorous, yet much more precise science of A/B testing.

The process of A/B testing is simply this:

1. Decide what feature you want to test. The variables you test could be anything from the color, shape, or size of a button to the precise wording of a call to action.
2. Create two versions of the same ad, landing page, app, etc. using two different choices for the variable in question.
3. Decide how long your test will run. I suggest at least two weeks, but it may be longer or slightly shorter depending on your traffic and industry.
4. Choose a testing tool to help you run your test. Some options include Hotjar, Crazy Egg, Optimizely, Adobe Target, AB Tasty, and Google Optimize 360.
5. Launch!
6. After a couple of weeks, take a look at the results. Which version won?
7. Rinse and repeat. A/B testing is most effective when done continually. That way, your marketing and digital presence can constantly improve, rather than only changing when things get bad or someone arbitrarily decides it's time.

Remember: Always Be Testing.

In this way you will learn *through hard data* what kinds of ads your customers respond to. You may be in for some real surprises. Maybe you *expected* your most lucrative customers to react better to ad A, but ad B brought in fully twice as much revenue for the same marketing budget. Aren't you glad you learned through testing that before you scrapped ad B entirely on instinct and poured your entire advertising budget into ad A?

A/B testing is huge in the e-commerce industry. Changes as small as the color of a button or the precise wording of a single sentence have been known to generate differences in conversion rates (we'll discuss exactly what those are next chapter, but suffice to say they're the major components of revenue and advertising ROI) of up to 50%. That's 50% more people taking a desired action because you used slightly different word order and punctuation, which you would not have learned without A/B testing.

Netflix understands this well. A 2019 release from GoodUI.org shows screenshots from Netflix's A/B testing of their landing page. Tiny variations in variables such as button size, font size, and overall page layout and features were tested to see which designs generated the most clicks.

The results were significant: Netflix discovered that making their "Try It Now" button bigger and more brightly colored had no positive effect on click rates, to the point that the marketing team decided to keep their old design rather than update it. It's unclear from Netflix's decision whether the bigger buttons they were considering implementing site-wide might have actually been *hurting* click rates, despite the intuitive logic that larger buttons should get more clicks. This is why A/B testing is so important.

Netflix's previous A/B testing had included findings that, for them, giving customers three choices to compare in the form of a simple checklist of features got more subscriptions than either offering only one option or offering a more elaborate information table comparing the options.[2]

Through A/B testing, online stores can increase the average order value, optimize their checkout funnel, reduce cart abandonment rate, and so on. There are nearly countless variables that can be optimized and tweaked, often yielding 10%+ increases in the desired customer behavior as a result.

You may try testing variables including:

- The way shipping cost is displayed.
- Whether and how the "free shipping" feature is highlighted.
- Text and color tweaks on the payment page or checkout page.
- The visibility and placement of reviews or ratings.
- How many screens the buyer has to click through to successfully complete a purchase. (Fewer is better.)

- Call-to-action position.
- Length of the page.
- Placement of video and credibility.
- Headline copy.
- Images.
- Message positioning.
- Number of form fields.
- Amount of copy.
- Offers.

A/B testing is so important that I want to take some time to discuss instances where seemingly inconsequential or far-from-obvious changes to an ad or website yielded *huge* changes in revenue.

AMAZON BREAKS E-COMMERCE WITH ONE BUTTON

The king of e-commerce optimization is, of course, Amazon. This retail giant has captured a frankly terrifying market share by anticipating ahead of the curve what online customers would want, and what would convince them to buy. Their immense dedication to providing the most convenient, comprehensive, and affordable shopping experience possible has led them to engage in high levels of A/B testing.

Arguably their most profound innovation has been the practice of "1-Click Ordering." By reducing the purchase process to literally a single click, Amazon has made buying from them far quicker, easier, and more convenient—and therefore more tempting—than almost any competitor.

1-Click Ordering dispenses with every intermediate step between seeing a product and actually giving Amazon money in exchange for that product. There is no need to give your address or payment info, since Amazon saves that information the very first time you purchase from them. There isn't even any need to display a "shopping cart" page, which both increases customer convenience and decreases the chance of customers second-guessing their desire to purchase or whittling their cart down in the checkout phase.

There are some trade-offs here: for example, Amazon won't let you purchase *at all* unless you make an account with them. Many online retailers, by contrast, still allow customers to "check out as guest," believing this will add to the convenience of making their first purchase. In reality, though, allowing "check out as guest" ultimately *increases* the burden of repeatedly entering information on the customer, and decreases their odds of becoming a habitual purchaser.

Amazon's ultra-streamlined "1-Click Order" also sometimes leads to potentially frustrating mistakes. What if the default payment method or shipping address on your account isn't the one you wanted to use for this particular order? Well, Amazon fixed that on the back end. If you realize a mistake has been made before your order is shipped, you can now go in and change the shipping address and payment method before it ships out. If you *don't* realize the mistake, Amazon can at least point out that you chose to use the added convenience of one-click shipping.

This approach to making it easier to buy than *not* to buy with a single click has proven to be so profitable that Amazon has even turned a profit on selling licensing rights to the formerly patented system. In 2000, Apple paid Amazon a huge sum for the rights to use 1-Click Ordering.[3]

Fortunately for you, Amazon's patent on 1-Click Ordering is now expired. You may wish to consider implementing a similarly streamlined system into your online store, or at least consider how you can cut out as much work and as many opportunities to second-guess as possible from your customer's online experience.

A 50% INCREASE IN ONE SENTENCE

One of the most striking examples of the power of a single, simple A/B test I've encountered happened while I was writing this book. A client was creating an ad designed to bring in new customers and their product team had suggested that we test two different version of the same phrase:

A. Get $10 off the first purchase. Book online now!

B. Get an additional $10 off. Book online now.

Now, which of those options do you think got more clicks in our test run? Which one do you think it was?

I, for my part, expected option A to do better. It has the amount of the discount closer to the beginning of the ad, fewer words for the reader to have to process, and the ad ends with more enthusiasm. If I had decided to forgo A/B testing and rely on my intuition alone, even as a marketing expert, I likely would have poured my entire budget into ads with phrase A.

Which phrase actually did better with our test audiences? Well, it was phrase B. And how *much* more cost-effective was phrase B?

Fifty percent. *Fifty percent* more people who saw ad B actually clicked on it and visited my client's website. That's three people for every two people the other ad brought in. In the long run, that could amount to fully 50% more sales revenue from an otherwise identical ad campaign.

Why was this the case? Maybe the word "additional" created such a strong sensation of saving *more* that 50% more readers could not resist.

But boy, we're glad we did A/B testing before allocating our entire budget to the option that *seemed* most correct. This is an excellent example of why A/B testing really is worth investing in, even if you (or someone on your board) is *sure* that they know the best way to advertise already.

EASILY BOOST CONVERSION RATES WITH THESE FEATURES

It might surprise you to learn that a few simple website features—features not directly involved in advertising or purchasing—can easily increase conversions and leads.

- Frequently Asked Questions address the most common concerns and uncertainties readers may have on the spot. Take this opportunity to address questions like your guarantees, return policies, and technical questions common to your industry. A website that answers a reader's precise question is more likely to get their business than a website that leaves them uncertain.

- Statistics make your product's benefits to the reader concrete. A documented 35% increase in revenue is better than saying "a big increase."
- Social proofs such as reviews, video testimonials, and case studies build trust.
- Go visual. A picture really is worth a thousand words as far as the information you can convey in an instant.
- Remove distractions to create a smooth, seamless experience on your website. If readers have to guess where to click next or concentrate to find what they're looking for, they're more likely to give up.

What do these features accomplish? Quite simple: they convince. Obviously placed statistics and social proofs demonstrate for customers the huge gains they could experience as a result of purchasing your product or signing up for your service.

And how do we know what formulas work? Because of A/B testing. Companies around the world have tested and tested to come up with precise estimates for what measures benefit conversion rates, because such figures allow companies like mine to demonstrate the concrete value of our knowledge.

Such figures *also* tell you exactly how to start increasing your revenue with a few easy adjustments. These website features cost little to implement, and they could increase your conversions from "viewer" to "customer" by a lot, or a little. You can only find out how much through A/B testing.

You can visit MiliaMarketing.com/Resources for a printable workbook including pages to help you with A/B testing.

CHAPTER 9
METRICS YOU MUST KNOW

KATHY AND TED were the owners of a family-owned cabinetry manufacturer and distributor that had seen astonishing growth in their early years. They'd started their business out of their home garage in the early 1990s, using Craigslist to advertise their wares to their community. By the late 2010s, they had a showroom, a national headquarters, and were doing roughly $15 million worth of business per year.

However, in the last few years, business seemed to have stalled. Old advertising tactics and processes weren't working anymore. While Mom and Pop Kathy and Ted were still immensely proud of the company they'd created, despair was starting to creep in. They knew they had the potential to do so much more—but they were struggling to compete with household names in the industry.

Would they ever have the big budget they needed to compete with the big names on advertising? Or would they always be regarded as a small fish in the national pond? These questions were starting to cause burnout for the family who ran this business. They were taking on more and more responsibilities to try to compete, but no matter what they did, nothing seemed to work.

What Kathy and Ted had discovered was that, as their business grew, *continuing* to grow required a fundamentally different skillset.

They didn't just need to ace the cabinetry quality and customer experience: they needed serious expertise in marketing, too.

When I first met Kathy and Ted, they were eager to try anything to break through the glass ceiling they'd found themselves facing as a small family-owned business.

- They didn't know how to identify where their biggest challenges were, or how to fix them.
- They didn't know what percentage of industry market share they held, or what percentage was held by their competitors.
- They didn't know how their website was performing.
- They didn't know where their leads came from.
- They knew they had to do something about it.

Our team met with Kathy, Ted, and other decision-makers so we could truly start from scratch. Early on, we analyzed their competitors and developed a long-term strategy accompanied by a short-term roadmap.

My team started with their website. Kathy and Ted had started their business in the days of dial-up: the time when text ruled the internet, images slowed load times significantly, and automation was largely unavailable to small businesses like theirs. Their website was crowded. It had too many calls to action, colors and photos were inconsistent, and it simply wasn't pulling any results that they were looking for.

Next, they had a target audience problem. Their first customers had been individuals looking to furnish their homes, but now they were in a position to sell in bulk. Architects, builders, and kitchen and bath showrooms made much more sense as a target audience, as people who may have millions of dollars at their disposal to furnish offices, apartment complexes, and more. We researched these target audiences and adjusted their SEO and ad keywords accordingly, targeting their ads and website so that they'd be shown primarily to people who were in the business of making big cabinetry purchases.

Like so many businesses, Kathy and Ted were, paradoxically, suffering from marketing budget inflation. They were buying radio,

TV, billboard, and newspaper ads—with very limited ways of tracking how many customers these were actually bringing into the store. When I met them, they were spending $25,000 per month on ads, and they had no idea how many purchases they were generating as a result.

This is a common situation for businesses that have recently started small and then grew. It can even happen to big businesses whose advertising and budgeting executives hail from the pre-internet era. There was little to no knowledge of online advertising techniques, no tracking of data to be used in optimizing future ads to be more effective, and so no way to truly optimize.

To make matters worse, Kathy and Ted had another obstacle to contend with: because their products were assembled in the U.S., they weren't the cheapest on the market. They were very high-quality. Kathy and Ted cared greatly about each individual customer who bought from them, and had created many jobs for American workers. But they weren't going to beat their biggest competitors on price point alone.

What could we do?

We started by making clear in their messaging *why* their products had higher prices. We focused on common pain points for bulk buyers: quality problems with the product, inability to contact the supplier to get these problems fixed. We guaranteed phone and email follow-up for customers who reached out via the website within 24 hours. We made the same promise regarding customer questions and complaints, offering a level of attention not available to most buyers from major global cabinetry dealers.

We promised, in short, a better and more supportive customer experience, even at a higher price.

Using FAQs, customer testimonials, and highly visual checklists comparing the attributes of their cabinetry to the attributes offered by their competitors, we made it very clear to customers who merely glanced at their website that Kathy and Ted could offer attention, customization, quality, and reliability that lower-priced competitors may not be able to. We planned all of this content to appeal to architects and kitchen and bath showrooms—bulk buyers who may spend orders of magnitude more than individual homeowners.

Now it was time to make sure that interested customers *saw* their website.

First, we focused on SEO. To compete at the national level, we wanted to optimize their website with keywords that would be seen by bulk buyers and not primarily by individual homeowners. We developed a long-term strategy to boost their SEO rankings with this group.

Next, it was time for ads. We targeted the same bulk buyers and created a plan to continually optimize our ad campaigns over time. In this way, I was confident that we could actually outperform the national giants: just like Kathy and Ted could afford to pay more attention to each individual client, they could spare more attention for laser-focusing their SEO and ad performance than the executives at the global brands were probably sparing to reach U.S. customers.

All that optimization paid off. Within the first 60 days of our paid ad campaigns, Kathy and Ted's ad conversion rate was 18%—10 times higher than the conversion rate of most pre-optimized ads! Their unpaid, organic web traffic had increased by 54%, and we'd counted 102 new leads that could be traced back to our improvements. This family-owned shop was now well on their way to continued growth and competition at the national level!

I tell you this because Kathy and Ted's success, largely, is the story of a journey from *not* knowing to knowing. Their early struggle was not due to any problem with their product or customer service, but rather to lack of knowledge about their ads, marketing, and website. At the beginning of their journey, they didn't know what web features statistically drive more sales; they didn't know how their competitors were advertising, and they didn't know how their advertising compared.

We changed all that by optimizing the metrics of success. And in this chapter, I want to tell you about some of those key metrics that you must know if you want to compete and trigger rapid growth.

RETURN ON AD SPEND (ROAS)

This is a metric that can be used as a gauge to monitor whether your ad spend is driving the expected value—especially as your campaigns scale.

The difference between ROAS is one of the most key metrics that needs to be monitored in A/B testing for optimal results. This simple equation—how much money is coming in on new sales for each dollar spent on advertising—is the first step to ensuring that your advertising is working *for* you and not against you.

The importance of ROAS is one major reason why I favor advertising methods where it is possible to closely track which purchases and customers are arising from specific ads. This is one reason why I advocate for ad-specific coupon codes or phone lines, and why I'm not a big fan of certain advertising methods such as billboards.

It's almost impossible to tell from a reliable, optimizable, data-driven perspective how much revenue an ad is bringing in if you're not able to track whether new customers or purchasers have seen it. Thousands of people may *see* an ad, but how are you ever going to determine how many of them decided to buy and what they bought unless you're using a tracking mechanism like a billboard-specific phone number?

That billboard may be the best thing you've ever done for your business, or you may be throwing away thousands of dollars per month for little to no benefit; there's no way of being sure unless you can track the relationship of that billboard to your subsequent sales precisely.

Fortunately, the world of digital marketing gives us very precise ways to track exactly how much we are spending per ad and exactly how much money each ad is bringing in. Two of the most important and commonly discussed metrics for online ads include...

CONVERSIONS AND CONVERSION RATE

If you've worked in any kind of sales, you know these terms. Typically, a "conversion" refers to the question of whether or not a *potential* customer who heard your sales pitch went on to become an *actual* customer who bought from you.

In the digital advertising world, "conversion" refers to when a user clicks on your ad and takes your desired action. When someone clicks on a Google Ad, lands on a page, and requests a quote. That's a successful conversion. Obviously, a higher conversion rate is better. A conversion rate of 100% means that every person who sees your ad or hears your pitch goes on to become a customer, while a 0% conversion rate means you are getting no benefit whatsoever from the ad you're running.

A successful conversion, such as an ad click, is not yet a sale. Converting an ad viewer into a customer usually requires several different conversion steps, which are collectively referred to as "sales funnel." When done right based on sound data and stellar design, sales funnels can generate effortless income for your business. When done wrong, mishandling of any step of the sales funnel can result in customer loss. That's why it's so crucial to invest in designing every step of your sales funnel, from the ad to the sales page itself.

Here are a few conversion rates that appear in your sales funnel that you will want to keep your eye on if you want to really optimize your business outcomes.

AD VIEW → AD CLICK CONVERSION RATE

In digital marketing, thousands or millions of people may have your ad load on their computer screen. Your optimization point here is your click rate: how many people are actually *clicking* your ad, indicating a strong level of interest in your product or service and giving you the opportunity to teach them more about it.

If your ad click rate is very low, that indicates that a more effective ad is probably needed to bring in new customers at the rates you'd like.

AD CLICK → INTERMEDIATE STEPS

Believe it or not, ads that demand the reader immediately buy from a company as the first step of the sales funnel often do *worse* than those which involve additional steps. This is because online shoppers are often hesitant to buy from a new brand they've just "met."

A sales funnel gives potential customers the opportunity to get to know a brand before deciding whether or not to purchase from them. This longer sales funnel often results in bigger and more repeat purchases than a one-time "buy now" button would alone.

Intermediate steps in sales funnels can include conversions such as:

- Potential customers give you their contact information in exchange for a new customer discount or a downloadable freebie. This step can be used to offer better deals to new customers precisely *because* they haven't done business with you before, or to show off your brand's expertise by offering a free download such as an e-book about your industry. Such free downloads that add value to the customer while allowing you to showcase your knowledge are called "lead magnets."
- Once you have the customer's contact information thanks to your coupon or lead magnet, you can send your customer email newsletters. If you make these interesting and engaging enough, yes, customers will actually read them and feel that they are developing a relationship with your team. They can also be used to invite customers to buy specific products from you at specific relevant times.
- The question of how many email recipients are actually opening your emails is another conversion rate you'll want to track. These hard data points can show without a doubt which email styles will generate more sales for your business, sometimes by orders of magnitude.
- Including sale links in your emails. As I mentioned above, the content you include in your email newsletters can (and sometimes should) include links to specific products and offers to make it as easy as possible for the customer to click "buy."

INTERMEDIATE STEPS → FIRST SALE CONVERSION RATE

How many people who click on your ad are actually going on to buy from your company? What are the weakest and strongest links in your ad → sale conversion chain? Can you use A/B testing or consult with an expert to learn how to strengthen your weakest links, drastically increasing sales success?

FIRST SALE → LIFELONG CUSTOMER CONVERSION RATE

How many people who make one purchase from you go on to make multiple future purchases over time? This is another great opportunity to spot red flags: if your rate of repeat customer business is low, could the problem lie in the quality of your customer service, or your product itself?

The good news is, digital marketing tools make it easy to track all of these metrics in great detail. Even the most basic online advertising dashboard generally shows ad view → ad click conversion rates for each ad you have run alongside additional detail about its target audience and graphics. With a little more engineering, the activity of potential customers *after* they click on your ad can be tracked to determine how often these people are actually buying your product. With just a little more engineering, you can determine how many of those who purchase based on your ad go on to purchase in the future, and how much they usually spend.

From this data, you can construct your holy grail of digital marketing: an ad campaign with a high conversion rate, which is specifically attracting customers who go on to become lifetime big spenders. This, just like all human relationships, is accomplished through understanding the best target audience for you and connecting deeply with them.

If your business already has a digital marketing presence, some questions you can ask yourself to improve include:

- Where, if anywhere, is your conversion rate failing? Is it your ads, your actual sales page, or your customer experience *after* purchase that seems to need the most attention?
- Are you attracting new customers, or returning customers? If you're attracting mostly existing customers, is there a

more cost-effective way to do that, or a way to more effectively bring new customers in? What's your customer retention rate? Your customer churn rate? Your net promoter scores?

- How many conversions are considered qualified leads? How many have a high chance of being profitable, and what do those potential customers have in common with each other? How can you target them more precisely in the future?
- How much in sales or revenue did your marketing net you in the past quarter, year, lifetime? How much did you spend on your marketing, and what was your return on investment?
- Keep in mind that your total advertising spend multiplied by your return on investment *is* your total revenue. This means that more advertising spend is generally better—as long as you've got a positive return on investment! Making sure you get a positive return on investment is what this book is all about.

THE KEY TO POWERFUL ADS

As you can see, the principle of knowing your customer—both through personal reflection on your shared values and experiences, and through data—reaches far beyond simple gifting programs.

Knowing your client inside and out will also help you when you implement this next strategy. In addition to building rapport through meaningful gifts that demonstrate your commitment to serving your customers, knowing your customer can help you to create a great experience for them each and every time a prospective customer interacts with your brand.

To gauge how well your ads are working, you can use the conversion rate worksheet found in the workbook available at MiliaMarketing.com/Resources.

CHAPTER 10
GIVE THEM A GREAT EXPERIENCE

YOU MIGHT HAVE NOTICED that the days of *just* offering a product to attract clients' attention are in the past. With providers from around the world competing to sell many of the same products and services, how can your business stand out?

One way to do this is to give customers an *experience* in addition to the base product. This approach echoes Boxed.com's extraordinary level of customer service, and it can be taken to the next level by businesses operating physical spaces.

Len Komoroski, former CEO of the Cleveland Cavaliers, understands this. His involvement in rethinking and redesigning his team's arena—now known as the Rocket Mortgage FieldHouse—was truly forward-thinking.

Len's thinking went like this: my team has a physical space. In fact, my team has a *lot* of physical space. In a pretty prime real estate area. What can we do with this *beyond* providing the traditional basketball-going experience?

Len understood that fans come to stadiums for *experiences*. The "traditional American basketball experience" is one of them. But what could Len add to that that fans couldn't get anywhere else? Even better, what could he add to the stadiums' capabilities that might make *other* businesses want to rent the space during the off-season?

Well, first and foremost, customer service. Just like Chieh Huang, Komoroski invested in warm, friendly, attentive, and personalized service. This vital emotional aspect of the customer experience was accomplished in the same three-prong way: by ensuring that employees were happy, well-trained, and supported by computer systems that made the technical aspects of their jobs as easy as possible. This model of producing great customer experiences through great organization and happy staff can be used by any business, online or physical.

As the steward of a physical space, Komoroski also had tremendous control over the guests' physical environment. For him, that didn't just mean luxury: it meant excitement and upping the space with the latest technological capabilities. Installing state-of-the-art lighting, sound, video, and computerized sensor systems enabled him to make the space *responsive* to the fans who walked through it. While watching lights and graphics respond to their presence helped fans to feel seen and important. The same technology made the stadium a highly appealing venue for other mass-seating events such as concerts visiting the city, bringing in additional revenue and adding to the fame of the location.

The updated tech also allowed Komoroski to excel in an important emerging area of customer experience: it allowed him to bridge the gap between the online and physical customer experience in new ways.

The Cavaliers are now famous for offering 360-degree virtual reality experiences, recorded in the stadium with their favorite team. By loading the programming onto VR headsets, fans who can't be there in person—or at least, can't be in the best seats—can access more of the stadium experience than ever before.[1]

This of course builds loyalty in addition to bringing in revenue. While we can expect that all of this may become the new industry standard in a few years, the Cavaliers have given themselves an edge by being one of the first sports teams to offer their customers this new technology.

DESIGNING YOUR ONLINE SPACE

Now, you may not be the CEO of a major sports stadium. You may not even have a physical space for your business. But there are still ways you can make the customer experience as enticing as possible—and build a reputation for an experience that's unique.

If you're a physical outlet, you can show customers that you understand them and value their experiences by providing spaces for things they love to do. One great example of this is Nike's decision to host mini-tracks and basketball courts at their stores to allow customers to get the best possible feel for how the product will perform for them before buying.[2] This does more than just demonstrate commitment to customer satisfaction: it also creates a *community space*, whereby the stores themselves may become a destination for reasons above and beyond the actual product that they offer.

Even if you don't have the budget to build a mini-track or basketball court, the basics may be easy to see: a pleasant, unique decor and nourishing freebies such as coffee, cucumber water, cereal bars, and phone charging stations have been a staple of material customer service for decades. These provisions cost relatively little and make customers feel cared for and comfortable. At a subconscious level, customers may come to subconsciously look forward to this experience of comfort and convenience in unique surroundings more than they realize. They may begin to find excuses to visit the space, even if they might not otherwise buy the product or take time out of their day to do so.

Now, what if I told you that a website could do the same thing?

The primacy of websites in the modern customer experience is the major reason why investing in good web design is so important. Whether *you* realize it or not, when your customer visits your webpage, they feel like they're walking into a room. Does that room surround them with a sense of color, comfort, or mystique? Does it make it easy for them to find what they're looking for, or to take the action *you* want them to take? Are there freebies, such as a small coupon or a free "lead magnet" available for new members? Is there a friendly "face" available in the form of an automated chatbot or online customer service agent who's available to answer their questions?

On the other hand, are customers faced with a wall of text that makes it difficult to find what they're looking for? Are they faced with endless menus, like wandering through a maze of rooms? Is the "decor" jarring, unattractive, or amateurish? If you have a website *and* a physical space, does the website show off your physical space in the clearest, most inviting way possible and make website visitors want to go there?

Customers are no longer using websites like books where they seek to read walls of text to expand their knowledge. Instead, customers experience websites like *rooms*: they are places with distinct looks and feels, which customers typically enter looking for something in particular and become turned off or frustrated if they can't find it easily.

Every business's fear when making their physical space as attractive as possible is that people may come to sit in their space for hours without actually buying products. To more than offset that concern, the "subscription" model which has proven so successful in the digital content arena has recently begun to spread to other industries. Businesses from bookstores to online clothing lines have found great success in offering "subscriptions" whereby customers pay a monthly fee for access to a members-only physical or digital space or a discounted rate on individual purchases.

The advantage of the subscription model is clear to behavioral scientists: people don't like to expend more energy than necessary. When we leave it up to them to make individual purchases, many won't. Subscriptions, however, take more money to *cancel* than to let run. Customers are more likely to decide to keep their subscription running, just in case they might need a product from you in the next few months, than they are to decide to visit your store and make discreet purchases at least that often.

Subscriptions can have the added benefit of acting like an online community space. If subscription customers are treated to curated content, private forums or social media user groups, and exclusive offers, the digital subscription space takes on all the trappings of a physical community space. And there's no reason to do just one:

subscriptions may cover physical *and* digital spaces and, if managed properly, will more than cover the cost of updating and running both.

You may not be the CEO of the Cleveland Cavaliers, but you can still have a website that feels like a unique, inviting space where paying customers can access friendly customer service, community with like-minded people, and, most importantly, can find the products or services they want to buy from you easily. Your website can still feel like a space that makes people want to stop, spend some time, and ultimately join up for freebies and access to exclusive content.

The customer experience is one of the best ways you can set yourself apart and make customers want to come back again and again, whether you're an online business or a physical one. This can be accomplished initially through gift-giving, but it must be sustained by designing a consistently comfortable and inviting space, whether digital or physical.

And there's one more thing you can do to cement your reputation in the minds of potential customers. When you make it easy for customers to learn from your expertise, you also demonstrate that you *have* expertise that your competitors might not have.

CHAPTER 11
DEMONSTRATE EXPERTISE

MUCH HAS BEEN WRITTEN about the art of in-person sales. One of the best talks I've seen on the subject was presented by Steve Nudelberg, a renowned salesperson, when he spoke at the Customer Service Revolution Conference hosted by The DiJulius Group in Cleveland. Nudelberg laid out the most important steps to winning customer confidence in in-person sales:

1. Show up. It really is true that 90% of life is showing up. If you keep showing up in the right places at the right times, eventually the right people will get to know you. You will become an insider in their world.
2. Have a routine and structure. Know exactly what your audience needs to know and tell them in the most effective way possible. Know how to lay out who you are, what you know about your customers' pain points and the information about how your product or service can solve their problem.
3. Have confidence. When you are confident that you can solve the customer's problem, it shows. When you have practiced or made this sale many times before, it shows. When customers can tell that you have a lot of experience making

> sales, that also tells them something else: that a lot of people have bought from you over a long period of time, and therefore your product must be good and reliable.

My own experience would lead me to add a fourth component to this list: relationship-building. Whether in-person or online, customers are more likely to buy from people they *like.* This effect can be especially powerful if you are someone who actually *owns* a business and who likes people or comes across as relatable.

People would rather buy from an individual who is friendly and takes the time to reach out to relate to them than from a faceless corporation that doesn't give them an individual to form a relationship with. Showing up on video yourself addressing customers, or hiring the right person to do so, demonstrates expertise in customers and relationships in addition to expertise in your product or industry.

You can't buy ad space for a live salesperson through Google Ads, but you *can* apply these proven principles to your online presence. Your website is your room, your space, the environment in which you want the customer to feel comfortable and enjoy themselves. It is also the room where they will meet your sales pitch.

Putting a great sales pitch into your actual advertising and sales copy is obvious. What might *not* be obvious is that there are also other ways you can demonstrate your expertise to customers through your ads and online presence. These methods are a special bonus of the digital space. They're all about allowing the customer to come to you for help and education on their own time, which is a luxury that in-person sales professionals don't have.

What are some ways you can create this friendly availability to customers without putting pressure on them to buy from you immediately? The answer is quite simple: you prove to them that you know how to solve their problems *by telling them how to do just that.* What are highly specific questions that your customers might have that your competitors might not tell them how to solve?

This might range from a how-to tutorial for a particularly bold or elaborate makeup or hairstyle to a breakdown of the pros and cons of various solutions to a financial quandary. Whatever your industry is, you *are* the expert, and you can prove that and give your potential customers a great experience at the same time by sharing the knowledge you think they might be interested in.

Now, some businesses are afraid to share too much of their trade secrets. There is certainly something to be said for the "secret recipe" that people can't get anywhere else, which sets your business apart from all others. But in many cases, there is little danger of customers feeling *so* well-informed that they don't want to work with you. In fact, when you show them precisely how to achieve the result they desire, who in the world are they more likely to trust to provide precisely the products and services they need to achieve the exact result you've now shown them is possible?

By building a stock of fun, inviting, frequently searched, and highly relevant videos or articles, you can build a relationship with the customer by answering their questions without having to spend hundreds of staff hours doing it. All you need to do is produce the article or video *once* and you can educate thousands or even millions of prospective customers without burning through thousands or millions of highly trained staff hours.

If you make your content sufficiently informative and entertaining, it can indeed become a form of entertainment that the reader will willingly indulge in for hours and hours while building their hopes and dreams for the future.

Sometimes, advertising a how-to video or article can be a great ad in and of itself. You're not obviously selling something, so the customer does not feel pressured or annoyed when they see your ad. Instead, if the article or video answers a burning question they have or looks colorful or beneficial, they may stop and take a look purely for entertainment without it ever occurring to them that it may end up giving them a hankering to buy.

The creation of these articles and videos is an excellent time to apply your in-depth knowledge of the customer. When you are seeking to (and hopefully hiring the expertise to succeed in) capture the customer's attention for a prolonged period of time, you have an opportunity to do far more than you could in a typical ad. You have the opportunity to connect with them at a deep relational level, if you can nail things like:

1. The customer's preferred communication style. For your target audience, does the customer want to feel like they're talking to their best friend, or an esteemed authority figure? Do they feel a deep respect and camaraderie with brands that use humor, or do they prefer a more stately and dignified personality? What speech patterns, language choices, or even regional accents do they prefer?
2. The customer's preferred entertainment and education habits. For your target audience, are they more drawn to entertaining or educational content? What kinds of YouTube videos are they watching? Which websites are they spending hours on, and what sorts of content do those websites host?
3. The customer's lifestyle. If you're selling a product or service that's directly relevant to lifestyle, obviously you want to know what *specifically* your most lucrative customers want to do with their money, or their beauty routines.
4. What might be *less* obvious is that not all of your content has to be directly relevant to your products and services. After all, not all conversations between human beings are about business. You may score major brownie points among your target audience if you take some time to provide fresh, fun recipes, "life hacks," or public service announcements about issues that are important to them even if these aren't directly related to your product.

Your online presence is your opportunity to build a relationship with your customer every bit as much as your physical product or location is. Don't waste it. Especially when standing out from your competitors on this front is often as easy as thinking outside the box.

If you're just getting started building or rebuilding your online presence, it's a good idea to prioritize the most obvious and direct aspects of sales. To reiterate, these are:

1. Direct ads and sales pitches constructed with an understanding of your audience, confidence, and structure.
2. A comfortable, inviting, easy-to-navigate online space that makes customers want to spend more time there.
3. Online resources such as videos or articles which may answer your potential customers' most burning questions.

Only after the above bases are covered, you may wish to start expanding your content production to include entertainment and other forms of brand and rapport-building that may not be directly relevant to your product.

CHAPTER 12
THE ULTIMATE STOREFRONT

YOUR WEBSITE'S landing page is one of the most important components of your digital marketing strategy. It determines how fun, easy, and appealing it is for an internet user who may have clicked on one of your ads or discovered you through an internet search to actually become a customer.

Your landing page is your digital storefront—and remember, as of this writing, most of *all* sales are conducted through digital storefronts rather than in-person storefronts. For this reason, it makes sense to put at least as much care into your landing page as you would into your physical space. The good news is, your landing page can often be more affordable, since you don't need physical real estate, architecture, or full-time staffing.

In this chapter we'll dissect what is, in my opinion, the simplest and most reliable formula to create a stellar landing page. This will be a landing page that invites users in with compelling imagery, promises to solve their problems, and provides credible evidence that you can in fact fulfill these promises all in a single glance.

What are the components of a stellar landing page?

THE FIRST THING YOUR CUSTOMER SEES

Any webpage can be divided into two major parts: what is immediately visible as soon as the webpage loads on the user's screen, and the additional content they discover by scrolling down. The top part of the webpage that is immediately visible as the page loads should contain a few carefully selected ingredients to make it as easy as possible for the customer to decide to buy or contact you within seconds.

It might not surprise you, then, that it's essential that the "above the fold" material clearly communicates what you are offering the reader. A visitor to your website is only likely to scroll down to view more if they are convinced from first glance that you can really help them.

Here's a list of components you will want to make sure your web design team includes at the top of the very first page readers see when they visit your site:

1. Explain what you are offering the page visitor. What value does your product or service create? What problem does it solve? Some examples might include:
2. End back pain.
3. Sell more online.
4. Fun for the whole family.
5. Explain *how* you solve this problem. What exactly is the nature of your product or service? For example:
6. End back pain with soothing tea.
7. Sell more online with search engine optimization.
8. Fun for the whole family at Joe's Steakhouse.
9. Address an objection. Like all good salespeople, digital marketers have to overcome objections which might cause a potential customer to initially fear that the product won't work for them. The best way to bring in customers is to address these objections directly in your copy above the fold. For example:
10. End back pain with soothing tea. No prescription necessary!

11. Sell more online with search engine optimization. Pricing options for every budget.
12. Fun for the whole family at Joe's Steakhouse. Free rib dinner for new customers!
13. Prove it. Anyone can *claim* to solve a customer's problems, and this means that most customers won't believe your claims unless you can offer social proof. This is where reviews, testimonials, and metrics come in.
14. As a general rule, it's a good idea to choose whichever of those options looks best. If you have hundreds or thousands of reviews averaging 4.5 stars or above, that speaks for itself. If you only have a few reviews at this point in your startup's life, using a few impressive metrics or a carousel of a few highly emotional statements may be better. For example:
15. End back pain with soothing tea. No prescription needed!
16. <Link to testimonial> "It changed my life…
17. Sell more online with search engine optimization. Options for every budget!
18. We have helped make 2,049 sales...
19. Fun for the whole family at Joe's Steakhouse. Free rib dinner for new customers!
20. <Link to 349 reviews with a 4.6-star average>
21. Make it visual. It's worth hiring a good illustrator or photographer to make your product come to life. Visuals can convey emotions and ideas that text alone cannot. Some examples might include:
22. For your soothing tea, a photograph of a person sleeping soundly or looking extremely relaxed.
23. For SEO, graphs or screenshots showing a sudden uptick in traffic, sales, or search engine rankings.
24. For Joe's Steakhouse, a photograph or illustration of a happy family having a great time with delicious food.
25. Call to action. Let's pause for a moment to appreciate everything your stellar landing page has already done. Within a fraction of a second, your potential customer has seen what you are offering, how it will make their lives

better, has seen proof that your product or service really works, and has seen a highly compelling visual showing what is possible for them if they become a customer.

26. Now it's time for a call to action. What action do you want your customer to take after viewing this impressive suite of information and visuals? Do you want them to buy right away? Do you want them to sign up for a mailing list to be coaxed into bigger or long-term purchases? Do you want them to download an app or a coupon that has been strategically designed to create loyalty?

The same rules we used above also apply here. We don't *just* want to ask the customer to take our desired action. We want to show them *what's in it for them* within the text of the call to action itself. For example, the text you place on the button that will take the customer to your online store, sign-up form, or download page could say:

1. Start Beating Back Pain Today
2. See How Affordable SEO Can Be
3. Get Your Free Rib Dinner Today

BELOW THE FOLD

Your goal with above-the-fold material is to help as many potential customers as possible to buy from you, give you their contact information, or download your app without even having to scroll down. But some potential customers will need more convincing. When they scroll down to learn more about what you have to offer, you want the information there to answer their questions and objections—and be just as compelling as the material above the fold.

To accomplish this as efficiently as possible, you'll want to:

1. Give additional concrete information about the value you offer. Address additional customer objections and share additional product features and metrics.
2. Here's what's in our calming tea. Here's how it works on

your nervous system. Here are clinical studies showing that these ingredients work.

3. Here are more customer case studies or impressive metrics from our SEO services. See exactly how much customers like you have benefited.
4. It's a good idea to make your case studies as similar to your *ideal* customer as possible, as the type of customer most likely to respond to case studies and metrics is the one who sees themselves the most in the examples you give, in terms of business size, industry, etc.
5. See all the delicious dishes and fun experiences we have at Joe's Steakhouse. Here are all the free promotions we have going on right now. See how much fun you can have as a new customer without spending as much money as you would elsewhere.
6. Remember not to allow these concrete features and metrics to take up *too* much space on the landing page. It's a good idea to display just two or three impressive facts, with the option for customers to click to get more details if they have a burning desire to continue to learn more.
7. You don't want to take up too much space on the landing page, because you also want to make it easy for customers to benefit from...
8. More emotional support. Share additional reviews and testimonials to prove that your product really works, and help readers feel the potential emotional benefit to them.
9. Here again, you can choose your most impressive review or testimonial, with the option for customers to click to read more if they have a burning desire to vet your social proof. But don't take up too much space on the landing page directly, because you also want your potential customers to find your...
10. FAQs to address any lingering objections or uncertainties the customer might have. How much does this cost? How long does it take? Does your product meet my dietary, religious, or ethical requirements?

11. Feature one or two of your most common FAQs on the landing page, with the option for readers to click to learn more. Don't take up too much space, because you want your reader's eye to stray to...
12. Start a personal relationship with a founder's note. A heartfelt, personal note from the business's founder to the potential customer reading this page goes a long way toward cultivating a long-term personal relationship with the customer.
13. Founders' notes are unlikely to win customers by themselves because, technically, anyone can write a heartfelt note. But once the customer has seen metrics and social proof and had their questions answered to their satisfaction, a heartfelt founder's note about the company's mission and vision goes a long way toward distinguishing your business from competition who may take a more impersonal or less mission-driven approach to providing similar products and services.
14. Now that your customer has had a chance to learn more about the product, have their questions and objections answered, and "meet" your founder, repeat your call to action toward the bottom of your below-the-fold content to make it as easy as possible for customers to decide to act now.

Following the sequence of steps described in this chapter is the easiest way to nail your landing page—your digital storefront, which is the first contact most customers will have with your brand.

Having these instructions in hand when you hire a web design team can help to ensure that their results are not just highly aesthetically pleasing and technically functional, but also laser-focused on bringing in new customers and building long-term customer loyalty.

CHAPTER 13
GO VIRAL WITH SHARING INCENTIVES

EVERY BUSINESS OWNER dreams of "going viral." Free publicity with little to no financial investment? Sign me up.

While there's no way to guarantee your online content will spread like wildfire, there *are* a few ways to improve your chances of virality. Let's take a few moments to discuss how to turn viral sharing into long-term profits, and how to increase your chances of going viral.

DON'T BUILD YOUR HOUSE ON RENTED LAND

It's a good idea for businesses engaging in digital marketing to use a mix of their own "digital real estate"—their own websites and mailing lists, which are immune to the whims of third-party service providers and therefore more stable and reliable—and social media platforms, where the business can take advantage of the work this third-party provider has done to draw in users for its own benefit.

One major goal of digital marketing is to convert users discovered through social media platforms into users of your own digital real estate, such as your company's mailing list or app. Since you have control over this mailing list and app, once you have converted customers from social media encounters to residents of your own digital real estate, you can be assured of prolonged contact with them no matter how social media apps might change their algorithms or advertising strategies.

In the making of this book I interviewed Joe Pulizzi, a marketing and content creation educator and bestselling author of a series of books on content marketing. One of his favorite principles is this:

"Don't build your house on rented land."[1]

Countless business owners and creators have found themselves devastated after seemingly small changes to their media platforms such as Facebook, TikTok, Twitter, or YouTube resulted in skyrocketing advertising costs or even complete loss of their audiences. That's why Pulizzi and other content marketing experts advocate strongly for prioritizing mailing lists that deliver content directly to users' inboxes.

While external platforms may be powerful tools to meet new people, cultivating a mailing list as a communication channel that your audience pays attention to guarantees that even if the worst happens and you lose your access to third-party platforms completely, the thousands of people with whom you've cultivated relationships over the years will be able to stay informed and maintain their access to your content through the channels you own and control.

And, of course, that means they'll be able to keep buying from you.

A mailing list under your direct control needs to be a priority for any business who wants direct access to customers. But to build a mailing list, you first have to find people who don't already know about your brand and impress them enough to convince them to sign up for more emails to their inbox. *This* is where social media comes in.

Used properly, social media has the potential to allow you to reach audiences of millions around the world, both through paid advertising and sharing of your content by those who already love your brand. Properly designed incentives can increase the frequency with which your existing customers share your brand with family and friends who are likely to be far more responsive to a referral or testimonial from a peer they know and trust than to a paid advertisement.

Before we move on to look at how to use these tools, I want to share a note of caution about the dangers of trying to do too *much*.

ONE PLATFORM AT A TIME

Reading about all of the tools at your disposal, it's easy to feel that your business should be doing *everything*, posting content to every social media platform, etc. But Pulizzi cautions that, as with all investments, it's essential to be informed and strategic about your social media investments.

"Right now," he told me in our interview, "the biggest thing I see with larger enterprises is they diversify too quickly. Instead of focusing on figuring out one platform to one audience, they are creating content everywhere. They create podcasts and webinars and TikToks and LinkedIn groups and more. With no focus, they just create a lot of mediocre content and don't build an audience on any channel.

"The better method," Pulizzi explained, "would be to master one platform first, and then once a minimum viable audience is developed, then the brand can create on other platforms."

After all, consistency is key for creating an audience who really feel they have a relationship with your brand. A strong relationship isn't built by someone shouting in the street to whoever happens to be passing by; it's built by someone sitting down with you at a coffee shop and taking a real interest in your life.

A business that spams multiple media channels with generic content is going to struggle to connect with anyone at all; but one who determines what online spaces their ideal customers frequent and dedicates time and resources to building relationships of trust will be able to make a lasting impression and entice potential customers onto their own "digital real estate."

Forming a connection with your customers through social media platforms will depend largely on the quality of your content. But the size of your audience and the budget and effort you must expend to be seen by millions will depend on your understanding of some more data-based, less interpersonal factors.

KNOW THE ALGORITHM

Every social media platform has its own unique algorithm for deciding which posts to show to which people. These can sometimes change without warning, which is one reason you want your ultimate goal to be moving audiences to your own digital real estate. As an advertiser growing your audience, your goal is to figure out those algorithms as much as you can and brew up posts that will be most favored by the algorithms that determine how many people see and interact with your posts.

The good news is, there are a few common principles all social media platforms have incentive to include in their decision-making process. Social media platforms also profit when their users love their content, so they will often offer free tutorials on what kinds of content are most likely to do well.

Principles that are nearly universal across social media platforms include…

LIKES AND SHARES MULTIPLY THEMSELVES

The more a piece of content is shared or commented on, the more appealing it must be. Therefore, posts that receive many views and customer interactions as soon as they are posted will be promoted to wider audiences from the very start of their lifespans. In the case of truly viral content, this principle can build on itself exponentially until a video or article has been shared millions of times within hours or days of its first appearance.

This means that if you can give your content a small boost in the first minutes after it is posted, this may translate into a huge boost in how many people end up seeing your content. Getting a dozen likes or comments in the first few minutes after posting tells the algorithm that this is a highly appealing piece of content that more people will enjoy seeing.

Don't cheat—all major social media platforms now have ways to detect fake accounts being used to give the false appearance of popularity to a post, and they may punish such behavior in long-term ways such as temporary or permanent bans. But if you can get a small team of real fans to comment on your new content in the first few minutes after it's posted, you can boost your content's visibility in organic algorithms across your platform.

TIMING IS KEY

Content posted during high-traffic times when your platform has many visitors is more likely to get an early boost in shares and comments, which can lead to virality. Social media platforms know this, and some, like LinkedIn, will provide automated suggestions for what time you should post content to get maximum views and engagements.

If your platform doesn't provide such recommendations, a little bit of research will surely reveal analyses of what the highest-traffic times are for specific social media platforms in specific time zones. Your own business may wish to conduct its own research into what days and times your specific ideal target audience is most likely to be using platforms and viewing any content that is posted in real time.

You can also use analytics to look into what times your business's content, specifically, tends to get the most views and engagements and schedule future content accordingly.

LEARN WHAT USERS RESPOND TO

Keep an eye out for platform-specific trends about text, images, and controversy. Most platforms, for example, favor posts with visuals such as images and videos over text-only posts when it comes to promoting posts to wider audiences. Some may keep specific records of how much text is too much, or what types of images and videos are most likely to attract shares and engagements.

It is also unfortunately a well-known principle of internet traffic that items sparking disagreement among viewers are likely to get more clicks and interactions, and subsequently more organic views, than those nearly everyone agrees on. While this principle must be handled with extreme care lest your content go viral in a *bad* way, it's a consistent enough principle to be worth considering in your branding.

These principles may vary from platform to platform, due to the differences in interface designs and mechanics between platforms. What works on Facebook will probably not be a best practice for Twitter or Instagram, for example, and vice versa.

Learn where your audience is—what platforms do your target income brackets, age ranges, and interest groups use the most? Then learn the best practices for that specific platform.

We'll cover multichannel marketing—how to mix social media with other communication and in-person platforms to become an integral part of your customers' lives—in a future chapter.

Knowing your algorithms can give your content an edge when it comes to virality. But for an extra edge on and off social media, you can…

INCENTIVIZE SHARING

The most successful advertising campaigns are often those which encourage users to produce publicity for you. One of the most brilliant examples of this in recent years has been Mercedes Benz's "Take the Wheel" campaign.

In this campaign, Mercedes Benz gave a selection of high-powered Instagram users a free rental of one of their luxury cars—with the promise that whichever influencer got the most "likes" on their posts about their rental experience would get to keep the car.

In one fell swoop, Mercedes Benz simultaneously recruited a huge amount of influence, minimized their costs by promising the big payout *only* to the winner, and incentivized their competitors to bring all of their own social media expertise, honed over the course of decades or years, to bear on getting Mercedes Benz as many views and likes as humanly possible. In the end, the car model upon which the "Take the Wheel" campaign was focused sold out before its launch date.[2]

You may not be a luxury car company who can offer a status symbol valued at $40,000 to whoever advertises for you most effectively. But you *can* incentivize both public and private sharing of your content, app, products, and services by offering rewards to members who successfully get you views, engagements, and ultimately new customers.

You may not have a fleet of luxury cars at your disposal, but if you deal in high-value products or services, you can still organize…

PUBLICITY CONTESTS

If you are a purveyor of products valued in the multi-thousands of dollars, holding a contest among influencers for likes and engagements may just be for you.

As always, carefully consider what your budget is and who you need to reach: do you really need to reach local people, or can you profit from attracting customers anywhere in the United States who have a specific need or interest? In that case, would you be better off trying to engage social media influencers with national or global audiences, or engaging the local community in some way, such as through campaigns involving physical coupons or members of the hyperlocal community?

When engaging influential locals in a contest, it may not be wise to pit them against each other and risk antagonizing their fans in your local area. Instead, you may wish to allow them to work cooperatively toward a shared common goal in addition to whatever personal benefits they may receive. A contest that gives local businesses the chance to win a fabulous prize for themselves, but which *also* raises money for a local charity based on the level of social media engagement, is a win/win for the local community and creates a reputation for your company as being a local benefactor regardless of who gets the most likes or comments.

When planning a contest for free items, it is important to note the difference between contest outcomes for high-value vs. low-value items. Holding a publicity contest in which competitors compete for a high-value item works well, because the incentive to perform well is huge and it's unlikely that most contest participants would have bought the item themselves without the contest intervening.

However, the reverse is true for lower-value items that cost less than $1,000. These items tend to be affordable enough that holding a contest to receive them for free may actually *decrease* your sales by causing potential customers to refrain from buying at this moment in hopes that they will later win the item for free. Because the cost is lower, the likelihood of each individual purchasing the item without a giveaway is higher, and it makes more sense to try to drive sales directly instead of incentivizing people to wait for the chance of potentially winning the item for free.

In addition, the lower cost of these items may mean that competitors in your contests don't put as much energy into recruiting publicity for you, further increasing the potential loss of sales from customers holding off.

If you're going to hold a contest for likes or clicks, make sure the item you are offering is of sufficient value that it isn't competing for customers who may be *more* likely to purchase from you if they are not holding out for a win, and that your incentive is large enough to recruit your customers' best behavior.

If your business model is not designed such that it's likely to benefit from the use of contests for publicity, you may instead benefit from...

PRODUCT DESIGNS THAT WORK BETTER WITH MORE USERS

Some products, by virtue of their design, inherently work better with more users. If you have designed a communication platform that requires a login to use, for example, your existing users will have innate incentive to invite others to join the platform so that they can use it to work together. Slack, Trello, and many dating apps fit this description.

Other products have other kinds of inherent incentives, such as fantasy football or the stock and cryptocurrency trading app Robinhood. With these apps, greater total investment in the users' favorite products automatically increases the value of the users' own holdings.

These incentives are built-in, but of course, it never hurts to remind users of them. In apps with these types of built-in incentives, messages reminding users to "share the love" or "make the app better for everyone" may not need to be accompanied by additional incentives to be effective.

A financial analysis of customer lifetime value and acquisition cost can help you determine if this next option might be right for your product as well.

FINANCIAL RECRUITMENT INCENTIVES

Many products offer direct rewards to customers in exchange for recruiting more customers.

Freebies, discounts, and financial rewards can be used to great effect to incentivize both new and existing users to grow your customer base. You may have already experienced products, for example, which offer a small freebie or cash payment to both you *and* your friend if your friend buys or signs up using a promo code you gave them. Such incentives can actually drastically decrease the cost of new customer acquisition by leveraging pre-existing social connections instead of throwing money at trying to attract the attention and win the trust of new customers as a total stranger.

Dropbox, PayPal, and Robinhood are among the companies which have offered free items, free or discounted account upgrades, and small cash rewards to customers who successfully recruit friends and family members to use their services. In many cases they have offered the same incentives to new members as a wise investment in cultivating customer loyalty.

These incentives may be the easiest to operationalize, because they don't require a specific type of product design that gets better with more users, or the kind of outstanding quality that sells itself. But, as you might guess, the ability to create an experience of outstanding quality is more powerful (if sometimes more difficult to achieve) than a mere freebie. Consider...

GETTING WORD OF MOUTH

The old adage in marketing is that good word of mouth can't be bought. It can only be achieved by a customer experience that is so unexpectedly good that the customer can't stop talking about it and trying to share the amazing benefits with their friends. While this is everyone businessperson's goal, the fierce competition to achieve it means that not everyone will succeed. Still, there are ways to improve your odds.

The DoubleTree hotel chain discovered one way to do this by introducing a cost-effective but emotionally powerful freebie: every guest is given a warm chocolate chip cookie at check-in.

This is an incredibly clever combination of elements. The financial cost of producing a single warm cookie is negligible compared to the cost of a hotel room rental, but a warm cookie conveys the sensations of "home," "care," and "pleasure" in such powerful sensory and emotional associational ways that this tiny investment blows customers out of the water. It is all the more powerful because it is unexpected: the customer was not *expecting* to get food value out of a hotel room transaction, but they were given this powerful experience anyway.

The power and unexpectedness of this experience has prompted spontaneous word-of-mouth publicity, with customers around the United States tweeting about their desire for DoubleTree cookies and the pleasure of checking in to find a warm chocolate chip cookie waiting for you.

DoubleTree's cookie initiative has become so popular that a completely separate arm of the business has spun off which sells DoubleTree cookies and shares cookie recipes for those who are not in a position to book a hotel stay but want the cookies anyway.[3] This cleverly creates the potential for an ongoing emotional connection and brand relationship with a company who may not otherwise have that opportunity, since hotel stays are a rare purchase for most customers.

User posts about brands on social media open up the potential for another form of viral incentivization, which is...

BE ENTERTAINING

Some products attract attention through digital presences that are so bright, colorful, or bizarre that viewers can't possibly miss them. Especially bizarre advertising may warrant social media shares simply by virtue of being "so strange I can't believe this is happening."

This is a marketing approach to be handled with care, because marketing through the bizarre and absurd can fall prey to a couple of common risks. One is that the bizarre content of the ad may actually distract from the identity of the product, leaving users widely sharing the ad but taking away no memory of what the ad was actually promoting. Another is that a product which is bizarre in ways that contradict the value of the product may be off-putting to customers.

On the other hand, going bizarre can pay off in big ways. Let's look at two examples of marketing campaigns that went viral through their sheer strangeness or absurdity, which caused viewers to watch the ads *en masse* sheerly for their entertainment value.

Quiznos was arguably a pioneer of this technique, harnessing a group of terrifying-looking singing rodents, harvested from an early internet entertainment site, for their "we love the subs" commercial series in the early 2000s. While some customers found the association of grotesque rat-like creatures with a food establishment so disturbing as to be off-putting, others were so fascinated by this bizarre choice that they watched the ads over and over and developed an emotional attachment to Quiznos as a company that shared their love of absurd humor and was daring enough to take a big risk.

Those who watched the ads over and over again internalized the catchy song sung by the bizarre photoshopped rodents, which extolled the virtues of Quiznos subs as being "toasty, warm, and crunchy." An undeniably appealing combination, even if it is being sung to you by some sort of photoshopped half-human marsupial.[4]

The marketing campaign of the body products company "Dr. Squatch" is arguably the spiritual descendant of the singing rodents. While Dr. Squatch toned down the grotesqueness by adopting the spokesbeing of an earnest, intelligent sasquatch, the combination of body soap and skin care with a mascot who is a hairy forest-dweller is bizarre enough to have entertainment value.

Commercials featuring various sasquatch characters extolling the virtues of various products have been so successful that they have been used by other brands such as Jack Links Beef Jerky and Purple Mattresses before Sasquatch found himself adopted as the full-time mascot of this (apparently very successful) soap and body care company.

All of these companies found that advertising through the bizarre appealed to millennial customers who place little importance on decorum and who delight in shattering expectations, and found that these ads were deemed so entertaining that young potential customers would often share them on social media and show them to friends simply for their entertainment value.

These companies also succeeded in making their products sufficiently integral to the plot of the entertaining story being told. Thus, customers tended to remember what the advertisement was for, avoiding the trap fallen into by some comedy-based advertising campaigns that succeeded in entertaining, but failed to impress upon the viewer why they should buy the product being advertised.

I encourage readers who are considering comedy- or shock-based advertising campaigns to look up some of the ads mentioned here to see how the use of bizarre and unexpected content can be combined with the traditional advertising methods of extolling and demonstrating a product's effectiveness. You may also wish to look up the viral Kitty Kommercial produced by Furkids Animal Rescue and Shelters to see how low-budget solutions can be just as effective in achieving virality through humor and entertainment value as expensive costuming and special effects.

MUTUAL PROMOTION

The master stroke of social media platforms is the fact that, every time a user promotes or shares their own content, they are simultaneously sharing and promoting the platform it is posted on. This is what has allowed platforms that make content creation and sharing easy to recruit billion-user customer bases with astonishingly small marketing budgets.

While you may not own a social media platform, it may be worth considering whether you can offer some kind of unique service users can make to generate entertaining or valuable content of their own—and advertise your product for you each time you share it.

Even if you are not primarily a content-sharing or creation platform, is there a feature such as a camera filter, trivia challenge, or short story contest through which you can assist users in creating content and then sharing them to social media—with your logo and a link to your app automatically attached by the sharing interface?

With just a little technical savvy, user urges to share entertaining, informative, and competitive content can be harnessed into organic social media shares. Properly designed, each share can invite users to download your app or visit your website in order to produce their own entertaining content or prove their prowess in a trivia challenge.

Later in this book, we'll discuss why you might *really* want to produce an app to promote customer loyalty, and why apps are among the keys to Starbucks's market dominance and Chick-fil-A's success. We'll discuss which business models benefit most from having an app, and under what circumstances possessing an app may be well worth the startup capital you invest in hiring a programmer and designer to produce one.

For now, we'll discuss one final way to increase your exposure without spending marketing dollars, by providing a different form of value to those who share your content. That is by...

ADDING VALUE

The Michelin star system of rating restaurant excellence is arguably one of the most successful marketing innovations ever created. Many people, upon hearing the term "Michelin star," ask, "Michelin, like the tire company?"

In fact, yes. The Michelin star rating system began as a promotion, invented by Michelin Tires, to encourage users to drive more and subsequently require more frequent tire replacements. Michelin's plan was to add sufficient value to the customers' travel experience by recommending the best restaurants to visit along their travel routes so that customers would happily pay for more tires in exchange for having some truly stellar dining experiences.

This is why the original definition of Michelin star ratings was based entirely around travel. Restaurants boasting a single Michelin star were worth stopping at if they were located along your route; restaurants with two stars were work making a special detour to attend. And three-Michelin-star restaurants were so good that they were worth undertaking an entire journey just to experience their world-class food and atmosphere.

This promotion subsequently spiraled into what is arguably the single most prestigious restaurant rating system today. Michelin stars are now viewed as *the* defining mark of accomplishment for a professional chef or dining establishment, and three-star chefs and restaurants are prone to become world-famous.[5]

Now, think about what Michelin has done here. They have created tremendous value for everyone involved: customers now have a reliable system for determining which restaurants will produce very good and truly mind-blowing cuisine, restaurants and chefs have a way to earn globally recognized distinctions for excellence, and Michelin Tires are mentioned every single time a customer or restaurant consults or boasts about the Michelin star rating system.

You may not have the influence to create a globally recognized system for rating excellence, but you *may* be able to create some certification or ranking system of your own that other businesses and consumers may be happy to consult and boast about. Can you give awards or ratings to other local businesses who may not have warranted the attention of now global giant Michelin, based on their quality of customer experience or their ethical practices?

As with the other tactics discussed here, this is a tactic to be handled with care. You *don't* want to alienate fellow businesses or customers by appearing to take on an unearned title of authority or superiority. But if you can offer useful, informative information to local customers, such as which local businesses engage in the most ethical business practices or provide the best value for their products, customers may appreciate the information enough to view it as a value add rather than a power play on your part.

These are just a few specific ways in which existing skills and social networks may be leveraged to obtain publicity for your company to obtain greater value than would be possible through a strategy of advertising to cold potential customers alone.

We've mentioned several potential tactics to draw in new customers in this chapter. Measures such as giveaways, creating an app, and more might sound like big investments up front, but we'll explore under what circumstances these measures will more than pay for themselves if handled properly in the chapters to come.

If you think one or more of these tactics may benefit your business, you can download and complete the printable workbook at MiliaMarketing.com/Resources.

CHAPTER 14
CONNECT AUTHENTICALLY

IN RECENT YEARS, the rise of social media as arguably *the* predominant form of entertainment has brought about an unexpected marketing revolution. This revolution, which goes beyond the way customers find media to alter what *kind* of media they respond to, has thrown many titans of the twentieth century for a loop.

Not long ago, a friend of mine expressed his puzzlement to me over the directions he'd been given by his marketing agency. This man, who had been making big decisions for his company since the early 1990s, had been asked to record an intimate message to his customers from his home office. And, to his bewilderment, he'd been specifically instructed *not* to use professional lighting or film equipment.

His marketing team knew what he, as an experienced marketer of a previous generation, did not. They knew that, in today's market, customers respond to realism, authenticity, and intimacy *better* than they respond to slick, big-budget productions in many cases.

In decades past, advertising production value was often viewed as an indicator of a company's financial soundness. If you couldn't muster the budget for a polished, visually stunning ad, the logic went, there must have been something wrong with your cash flow. If your product was really that great, you'd have been able to afford a higher budget for your commercial.

This all changed over the course of the past decade, as one-on-one video communications gradually became a ubiquitous way for anyone —rich and famous or otherwise—to directly address their followers through social media. Fans soon delighted in seeing celebrities and major corporations communicating with them in this intimate way, as though they were equals and friends.

Indeed, social media has done a great deal to level the playing field for small businesses, and to challenge big businesses to cultivate more equal relationships with their customers. The previous century's sensibility that aloofness and inaccessibility made one seem powerful and mysterious has largely been replaced by a sense that, if you really care about your customers or fans, you will communicate with them as equals. The sensibility that successful companies should have polished big-budget ads has been replaced by a sensibility that too much polish can indicate emotional distance in a bad way.

Now, I want to be clear about one thing: looking like you're *trying* and failing to have high production values is still read as a red flag by modern audiences. Trying and failing to achieve the big budget look combines the worst of both worlds: it shows that you are trying to act superior to your audience and put on a front of wealth and skill, but you don't actually *have* the wealth or skill to pull it off, which suggests that you are neither a purveyor of quality nor a business that seeks to intimately relate to its customers.

This is why my friend was instructed to make his video the same way most social media influencers do: using an ordinary, everyday webcam, ordinary lighting, and the real, authentic environment of his home office for the message. This ad was meant to be an invitation to an intimate relationship with his brand, and a willingness to let customers see the genuine personality behind the scenes.

There is still a place for big-budget video advertisements, of course, but that role is shrinking as the role of personal addresses, endearing low-budget ads (most of the wildly successful Sasquatch ads in the previous chapter, for example, were not what we might call Hollywood-level productions), and personal testimonials grows.

In this chapter we'll discuss several specific case studies of times when authentic, personal communications from a company, founder, or random internet user far outstripped the more professional, polished, high-budget competitor.

There is still a time and place for big marketing budgets. But make sure you're investing where it counts—which, for my money, is primarily in ad targeting and responsive web design, not in big budget ad production.

To get an idea of how this works, let's look at a few examples collected by MarketingExamples.com.[1]

THE POWER OF AUTHENTIC ENDORSEMENTS

One of the most powerful illustrations of the shift from customers preferring prestige to preferring authenticity comes from bestselling author Nassim Taleb.

Taleb, turned off by the emotional distance and carefully polished statements of prestigious reviewers like The Economist, decided to replace the words of established media empires with reviews from real readers in his recent marketing campaign. Let's take a look at one of the reviews he selected to publicize when advertising his new book:

> *"The problem with Taleb is not that he's an asshole. He* is *an asshole. The problem with Taleb is that he's right."*
>
> *—Dan from Prague, Czech Republic*

Now, doesn't that make you want to read Taleb's book *more* than a prim and proper review quote from *The Economist?*

You don't need to know who "Dan from Prague" is. You don't need to know because he's not just telling you how *good* Taleb is. He's telling you something far more interesting. He's telling you that Taleb is an asshole, but still so inescapably correct that his assholery doesn't matter. The idea that Dan is an average reader just like you, not a magazine editor with decades of experience, may actually make Dan's testimony *more* interesting.

Now that Dan has told you that an average person like yourself finds Taleb to be inescapably right even though he's an asshole, you must know what Taleb is saying.

Or at least, that's my reaction.

RIHANNA KNOWS WHAT'S UP

The problem with best practices is that, after a while, they become cliche. It's probably safe to say that 90% of makeup brands advertising today use similar approaches to ad copy: the use of glittering generalities, superlatives, and words that evoke images of status and beauty to convey that their product will bestow status and beauty upon the buyer.

The problem with this is that, at this point in time, these tactics have become so ubiquitous that many customers automatically filter out such product descriptions as being obvious ad copy. Such descriptions feel generic, and worse, salesy. The reader knows that this copy has been written by someone tasked with selling to them at any cost, regardless of how good the product actually is. This faceless corporation has ulterior motives and can't be trusted.

This is arguably one reason why Rihanna's beauty and clothing lines have been exploding in recent years. Rihanna understands her fans, and the sorts of people who buy her products. She rose to fame in the era of social media and made a name for herself as an artist whose lyrics extoll the virtues of loyalty, friendship, and authenticity over status symbols or false glamour.

When Rihanna advertises her own product launches, she does it not as a polished, corporate identity, but as a friend confiding in her peers:

> *"Ima try my best to be humble about this, but @fentyskin is coming out July 31st exclusively at FENTYSKIN.COM! Y'all ain't hear it from me, but you can shop early if ya drop me your email at rihanna.io/fentyskin."*

Rihanna makes several key choices here that not only distinguish her from her competition, but mark her as more trustworthy and more worthy of support than her big competitor brands.

By choosing to use vernacular slang instead of dictionary-perfect English, Rihanna marks herself firmly as a member of her target audience. She is not some editor or executive sitting in an office somewhere, striving to meet the class norms of the rich and powerful: she is a young person who lives in the real world and is genuinely excited to launch a new product line based on her passion, and designed to meet the needs of others like herself.

You trust Rihanna because you get the impression that she really cares about doing a good job, and you want to support her *because* she is new at this, not a long-established big business.

You get the feeling that if you Tweeted at Rihanna with a question, concern, idea, or bad experience, she might Tweet right back and act on your feedback.

And indeed, engaging in exactly that sort of one-on-one social media interaction with fans has been a key ingredient for several big brands looking to build a viral loop into their advertising. When major brands and celebrities Tweet back at ordinary people—especially when they respond with genuine, witty, and unique language—these Tweets can be screencapped and circulated for months across social media platforms by fans who appreciate the humor and personality of these social media accounts.

Increasingly, informality and accessibility—not formal polish and prestige—are the name of the game in cultivating relationships with customers who grew up with the accessibility and genuineness of social media rather than the professional polish of TV.

REAL PEOPLE, REAL VOTES

In 2019, the People's Vote Campaign spent more than £800,000 to encourage people to vote in the 2019 U.K. election. Most of their budget went to producing traditional, high-end ads with expensive lighting, cameras, editing, etc..

The People's Vote Campaign learned a lesson worth tens of thousands of pounds when they released an ad that had been simply shot on an iPhone in selfie mode, featuring a People's Vote staff member speaking sincerely from the heart about what was at stake in the upcoming election.

This ad, which cost virtually nothing to produce but brimmed with authenticity as one citizen spoke to another about why they cared about the election, generated more engagement and more social media shares than any of their slick, professional, big budget ads of the past.

The message was clear: people care about *people,* not about corporations. Companies flexing what were once considered status symbols of corporate success could now connect with customers more effectively by sharing their most genuinely valuable asset: the real people who make their operations tick.

AN AD THAT DESERVES A SPOT ON THE FRIDGE

Perfume commercials are, traditionally, the epitome of status symbol ads. A typical perfume ad involves an A-list celebrity wearing an outrageously expensive designer wardrobe while partying in a high-class locale. The message is clear: buy our product and you can have all of this class, beauty, and mystique.

It was rather radical when, in 2019, Chanel decided to commission a bunch of elementary school kids to create their latest ad campaign.

The ads, designed to sell perfume as a Mother's Day gift, replaced high-end photography with crayon drawings of their perfume products done by employees' kids.

Seeing these images in the slots normally occupied by images of wealth and status sent a powerful message to customers: Chanel wasn't *just* the perfume of the glamorous and powerful. It was also a perfume created by people who had children, and who sought to make mothers everywhere feel like A-list celebrities partying it up in Paris.

When you put it that way, Chanel's sometimes upper-class price tag starts to look downright reasonable as a way for mom's partner and kids to make her feel like a queen. And this effect could never have been achieved without the kids who reminded everyone that Chanel can be for everyone.

DON'T SHY AWAY FROM AUTHENTICITY

It probably goes without saying that trying to manufacture fake authenticity is likely to backfire spectacularly, just like trying to make a big budget ad without the budget to do it properly. Trying and failing to project a specific image is one of the worst things a brand can do in marketing, because it feels deceptive. Customers who don't believe you are who you say you are based on your ad are unlikely to believe you about anything else.

However, the great thing about authenticity is that we all have it. It doesn't have to be purchased, learned, or competed for.

We all do what we do for a reason. Hopefully, most of us have at least a little bit of genuine excitement for our company's mission and vision. If we *don't* have genuine excitement for our products and services, it's time to rethink our products and services from the ground up. After all, it's virtually impossible to make customers excited about a product and a brand that *we* are not excited about ourselves.

To access our authenticity, all we have to do is learn not to be afraid of the camera. Gone are the days when impeccable lighting, makeup, and a script written in dictionary-perfect English were necessary—or even a good idea—for our ad campaigns. Customers in the social media era want to do business with people like themselves, *not* big businesses that rule from a television studio somewhere.

Break out that smartphone or webcam. Turn on selfie mode. Prepare like you're getting ready to talk to a friend; *not* like you're going to a board meeting. Try recording a short, sweet message from the heart.

I promise, your customers care more about who *you* are and why you do what you do than about the fanciest cameras money can buy. And they'd rather be your friends than your shareholders.

You can brainstorm some ways to connect authentically to your customers with the worksheet found in the workbook at MiliaMarketing.com / Resources.

CHAPTER 15
WHAT'S YOUR RETURN ON EXPERIENCE?

IN THIS CHAPTER we're going to examine three case studies from among The DiJulius Group's biggest clients, and then I'll share the DiJulius formula for customer service, which any business can utilize.

Before moving forward, you may wish to flip back to Chapter 2 and review the FORD questions we looked at for use in building your customer personas and customer journeys. FORD questions are useful in nearly any business setting that involves relationships, and you'll see how they were put to use in the examples below, where unique and highly successful solutions were designed around an intimate understanding of each brand's customers.

Remember: the best marketing in the world can't compensate for poor customer service, as word of mouth is stronger than any paid ad. But promising and then *delivering* an amazing customer experience can allow a new startup to rapidly outpace Amazon, as we've seen with Boxed.com. Let's look at a few case studies of ROI from improving customer experience that have been collected by the DiJulius Group.[1]

STARBUCKS'S 44% EARNINGS BOOST

Starbucks came to The DiJulius Group seeking a solution for the apparent flag in customer enthusiasm. To the experts with DiJulius, the problem was clear: the brand had become so focused on gobbling up market share during its rapid growth that it had begun focusing on the quantity of customers served and lost sight of the *quality* of the customer experience. Its staff training developed in the late 2000s emphasized speed and accuracy of product delivery in the face of the long lines of the pre-recession customer boom, but mere speed and accuracy do not make for a caring or soulful customer experience.

The DiJulius Group could see what Starbucks's customers really wanted. The brand had developed a reputation in its early decades, not just for coffee that tasted good, but for its associations with the centuries-old concept of "coffee shop culture," where coffee shops did not merely serve coffee, but also acted as community spaces for warm interactions and intellectual conversations.

Reducing the products they served to a merely clinical matter of combining the right ingredients for delivery within 90 seconds had reduced baristas' enthusiasm for their jobs. Merely mixing coffee ingredients to meet time quotas, after all, does not feel very inherently meaningful; it does not feel like the kind of job you invest your heart and soul into. Customers sensed the difference.

The DiJulius Group crafted a new mission statement for Starbucks in 2010. The new mission was "To inspire and nurture the human spirit one person, one cup, one neighborhood at a time."

That's more like it. In this way, The DiJulius Group shifted the focus of every employee in the company from mere speed and technical correctness—important concerns, and easy ones to measure, but perhaps *less* important than the "coffee shop spirit" that brought millions of customers through coffee shop doors each day to get a taste of not just espresso, but also warmth and inspiration.

The job of a barista feels more meaningful, rewarding, and challenging when nurturing the human spirit is its primary goal. So, for that matter, does the job of a coffee roaster. Every employee in every company wants to make a *meaningful* difference in the world, and emphasis on quotas and technical correctness can obfuscate the beauty of a job that is done not merely adequately, but *exceptionally* for the customer, who gets to experience an excellent product from the hands of a caring artisan.

How does one implement the vision of "inspiring and nurturing the human spirit?" The new mission statement came with four guiding principles:

- Anticipate—This pillar encouraged Starbucks staff to observe individual customers and anticipate their unique needs. Does this person look like he needs to be in and out as soon as possible, or do they look like they could use a kind word and a big smile? Do they look like they're settling down to enjoy the cafe atmosphere, or like they're rushing off to a big meeting?
- Connect—When possible and appropriate, make personal connections with customers. Having a warm, supportive conversation may sometimes be more important than having the drink ready in 90 seconds flat. If there's an opportunity to get to know regular customers, do your best to get to know them personally.
- Personalize—Each drink comes with the customer's name attached, and the possibility of nearly infinite personalization. If you have time to draw fun latte art, that can enhance the customer experience as well.
- Own—Starbucks encourages its employees to own the customer experience, even authorizing staff to replace spilled drinks at their discretion if it means creating great word of mouth for the franchise.

Customers picked up on the difference the new mission statement made. In the months to come, total earnings rose 44%. Customer visits increased by 5%, and more customers were paying for more expensive items, reveling in the sense of luxury that now made a Starbucks visit more than just a utilitarian transaction.

How can you incorporate these principles into your marketing? Remember, marketing must be congruent with the customer experience to get great word of mouth. Sometimes it takes the eye of a marketing team to spot what customers are *really* looking for, which may sometimes be a culture or experience that completely transcends the company's physical product.

Your job as the marketer is to identify what it is that your brand's best customers *really* want and then make sure they get it. This can include pushing for changes to customer service and other areas of operations. The only way to generate great word of mouth is by ensuring that the experience of customers on the ground matches the great experiences you show customers in your ads.

DOMINO'S HIGHEST CUSTOMER SATISFACTION SCORE IN HISTORY

Starbucks was not alone in discovering that focusing on speed and accuracy did not always yield a better customer experience. In the late 2000s and early 2010s, RPM Pizza (the largest franchisee of Domino's Pizza) focused on developing best-in-class speed of pizza delivery, based on the logical assumption that faster delivery would translate to happier customers.

However, in 2011 a mystery shopper survey revealed that RPM Pizza actually ranked *last* among major pizza delivery brands in hospitality, despite having the fastest delivery speeds on average. What was going on here? Based on the Starbucks story above, you may already be able to guess.

Pizza is inherently a social food. It is designed to be shared between at least two or three people, and to be delivered under circumstances where the people in question do not want to cook for themselves. Is this because they're partying and having a good time? Because they're having a busy day, or because something has gone wrong, leaving them too stressed to cook? It could be any of these things.

That's why The DiJulius Group produced a half-hour video for RPM's executives and staff, illustrating what may have been going on in a customer's life before they ordered a pizza. In most cases, the common denominator was that people ordered pizza because they wanted to spend quality time with their loved ones while eating a comfort food.

This operation gave birth to a new company mission statement: "Creating smiles by making lives easier." Like Starbucks's rethink, this mission statement refocused every employee at RPM from merely technical details such as delivery times and onto the emotional and social circumstances of their customers. Personal attention, RPM's case graphically illustrated, was more important than more easily measurable factors such as delivery speed.

Creating and delivering a pizza was no longer merely about the mechanical assembly of ingredients: it was now about making someone's day better. It could be about participating in festive occasion, or about giving a pick-me-up to someone who was experiencing stressful circumstances.

By 2013, RPM's customer service culture had transformed completely. Sure enough, their satisfaction ratings had reached record levels for the company.

CARTER MARIO LAW FIRM DOUBLES WORD OF MOUTH

Carter Mario is a law firm specializing in personal injury in the state of Connecticut. When the law firm first started tracking its referral sources in 2006, 30% of referrals came from word of mouth while 70% came from paid advertising. They wanted to improve that ratio, for two reasons. I want to spell those reasons out here because both are relevant to your company's long-term strategy:

1. Word-of-mouth referrals are often regarded as the gold standard for marketing and business success. Nothing signifies customer satisfaction better than customers recommending your brand to friends and family, without having to be prompted or materially rewarded for doing so. Great word of mouth supports your marketing because people are far more likely to click on an ad for a brand they've previously heard good things about from trusted friends. Great word of mouth also signifies that everything is going right with your company from the customer perspective.
2. Paid advertising costs money. This may be obvious, but this implies that improving word of mouth saves money on

advertising in the future by creating positive brand recognition and unpaid new customer recruitment.

So how could a law firm improve its word of mouth, given that law firms are not in a business model that can easily offer free samples of their product to the public at low cost, and few members of the population were likely to need or benefit from their services at any given time?

In the case of Carter Mario's clients, the primary product on the table is of course good legal services leading to positive legal and financial outcomes in cases of personal injury. However, just as with Starbucks and Domino's, what the customer *really* needs in the moment they interact with the law firm goes well beyond technical proficiency. These are people who are hurting and probably feeling frustrated, ignored, and vulnerable. There are things a law firm can do to help these customers feel cared for, seen, and supported that go far beyond the firm's technical prowess in the courtroom.

The DiJulius Group also created a new service vision with a focus on making a meaningful contribution to their clients' lives, similar to Starbucks's and RPM Pizza's, and a list of "always" best practices and "never" forbidden practices for Carter Mario employees. Knowing that customer interactions with a personal injury law firm were likely to be part of a long and challenging customer journey, The DiJulius Group also created a journey map to identify key points in the customer's personal injury lawsuit journey and identify how the law firm could anticipate and provide emotional as well as material support at these key points.

Some support measures the law firm decided on included:

- A Carter Mario team member staffs the phone lines 24/7. Customers dealing with the sensitive and frustrating matter of a personal injury that negatively impacts their life should never get an answering machine.
- If calls from clients were not returned the same day, Carter Mario himself would treat them to lunch.
- Every morning, a "huddle" between staff is used as an

opportunity to exchange information, both personal and technical, about the day's anticipated clients.

- The front desk is never left unattended.
- Any staff member who comes within five feet of a client is trained to smile, make eye contact, and say "hello."
- Clients are offered free Carter Mario umbrellas during poor weather. The production cost is minimal, and the emotional impact of feeling that the company has their back is enormous.

Over the next six years, the effect of these innovations was tracked. By 2012, a full 60% of the law firm's new business came from word of mouth, with paid advertising now supplying only a minority of new clients.

It's easy to see how the changes made to Carter Mario's policies allow the firm to go above and beyond for customers who are likely to be working with their brand long-term while experiencing a frustrating and vulnerable situation. Feeling that their law firm goes above and beyond to have their back doubtless leads to many unsolicited stories told around coffee tables, and to quick referrals when Carter Mario clients learn of friends, family members, or colleagues who are suffering as a result of personal injury.

CHAPTER 16
WINNING WITH MULTICHANNEL MARKETING

WITH AN EVER-GROWING list of ways to contact and engage customers, using just one method is often not enough to beat the competition. That's why more and more brands are turning to "multi-channel marketing"—the practice of using a strategic mix of online presence, mobile app presence, and in-person locations to help customers buy in the way that is most convenient for them.

The four pillars of a typical multichannel marketing strategy include:

1. A website to take online orders from web surfers.
2. A social media presence to keep your brand's voice active in people's lives as they go about their daily scrolling.
3. A mobile app or highly mobile-friendly website to enable customers to purchase everything they need right from their phone screens.
4. In-person locations that integrate with the other components to make the customer's experience as convenient, streamlined, and personalized as possible.
5. (Optional bonus) Direct-to-consumer emails and text messages can be highly influential additional components to

help ensure that users get to see special offers and updates from your brand and are reminded of you frequently.

On the surface, this may sound like a lot of duplication of effort. Why expend the necessary resources to allow customers to order from a computer *and* from a mobile device *and* from an in-person location?

The answer is one we've discussed earlier when discussing the wonders of the "Buy Now" button. The easier you make it for consumers—*all* consumers, no matter how they find themselves interacting with or thinking about your brand—to buy, the more of them will do it. Even requiring a few extra clicks, let alone requiring a customer to go home and get on their computer, or physically walk into a store, can cause the customer to lose enthusiasm and abort their purchase.

And well-managed multichannel marketing does not involve mere duplication of effort. Instead, all of your distribution and advertising venues can work together to create a whole that is greater than the sum of their parts and helps customers feel good about doing business with you. Let's look at two examples of highly successful multichannel marketing approaches below.

APPLE'S CUSTOMER SERVICE CENTERS

I'd like you to take a moment to think of an Apple store. If you've been inside one in the last five or 10 years, think about how it felt to walk into one. How did you feel while you were there? How was this experience radically different from the experience of walking into, for example, Best Buy?

If you're like most customers, walking into an Apple Store probably felt *very* different from walking into a standard electronics retail store. For one thing, Apple stores are carefully designed to feel futuristic, as though you have walked into a place where the impossible becomes possible. But probably the biggest difference is this: you may have noticed, if only subconsciously, that the pressure to buy a product on the spot, which is a common feature of traditional retail outlets, was almost entirely absent. If you're like many customers, this may have set you at ease and helped you feel more comfortable going back.

This remarkable situation is the result of Apple's skillful use of a multichannel marketing ecosystem. Realizing early that online purchases were the future, Apple shifted almost all of its actual *sales* to its online presence years ago. Apple figured out before most retailers that most customers would probably prefer to be able to buy *whenever they felt like it,* without having to physically go anywhere to complete their purchase. Products could be bought from any device, shipped to the customers' door—and only if there was a problem would the customers need to make an in-person trip to the store.

The Apple Store, then, became *primarily* a customer care hub, not a sales point. While this strategy may have seemed nonsensical to Apple's competitors 10 or 15 years ago, to modern eyes it's brilliant. Apple simultaneously made it incredibly easy for users to make impulse buys on the spot and ensured that they had a well-stocked network of expert customer care and technical support staff available to customers in-person all through regular business hours around the country.

Apple's stores were supported not by direct on-site sales revenue, but from the online purchases made by faithful customers who stayed with the brand because of the unparalleled ease of accessing expert support. The happy side effect of a lack of in-store sales pressure made it easier and more pleasant for customers to walk into Apple stores, ask questions, and get to know the products without experiencing pressure to buy on the spot. After all—there's no need to buy at the Apple store when the brand *expects* you to buy from the comfort of your own home.

Contrast this to the often-frustrating model of traditional big-box electronics stores. Many of the brands they carry are difficult or impossible to buy directly from the manufacturer online. If something breaks, finding an expert who knows how to take care of the problem can be time-consuming, and stores sometimes fail to have staff on-site who can handle the problem. The sensation that customers are expected to spend money at every visit to the store does nothing to make them want to return. It's a completely different experience from that of Apple's customer care centers.

Of course, Apple's online ordering and in-person stores are only two components of its richly integrated ecosystem. Apple also offers multiple apps, which they have done their best to make indispensable to their users' daily activities, such as streaming music. And these apps also act as data collection and communication channels, allowing Apple to push new content and offers and collect personalized data about customer habits.

Apple has also embraced the subscription model for many of its services, which is seen as the wave of the future by a growing number of retailers and service providers across industries. Even restaurants, bookstores, and clothing and cosmetics brands are now offering subscription models, which actually make it more difficult to *refrain* from buying than to buy.

The idea of subscriptions is that you pay a recurring monthly or annual fee up-front in exchange for special access, discounts, or content. By purchasing a subscription, or a "membership" as some retailers are calling these programs, you give the brand money up-front with the expectation that the fee will ultimately save you money or deliver you valuable content over time. Of course, this motivates you to make additional purchases using your specially discounted price or reward points system. These services can provide truly excellent values for devoted customers while simultaneously building brand loyalty.

But the real win for the brands is that they win even if you *don't* make further purchases. It takes more effort to cancel a subscription than to leave it running, which means the brand is more likely to obtain recurring payments from you than if they relied on you to independently decide to make multiple separate purchases in the absence of a reward program. This is why so many brands are now adopting subscription and membership models, regardless of industry. The greater ease of purchase offered by advancing technology is facilitating this trend.

Critics say that Apple has even gone too far in rendering customers dependent on their specific hardware by designing apps that will, in some cases, run *only* on Apple machines and content that can be accessed *only* using Apple hardware and software.

Such practices on the part of tech giants have come under increasing legal scrutiny in recent years and may soon face anti-trust lawsuits in courts around the world. But we can nonetheless learn from them the general principle of encouraging customer loyalty and interaction with your brand by offering perks that may be useful in daily life, and that *only* your brand can supply.

STARBUCKS'S BRAND ECOSYSTEM

We've already discussed in previous chapters how Starbucks has made excellent use of buy-one-get-one-free offers, loyalty programs, and other app features to cultivate customer loyalty and convert new customers. However, this is only scratching the surface of what they have accomplished using their store-app-website ecosystem.

Starbucks stores are clearly where most Starbucks sales are physically completed, but today many Starbucks purchases begin online or in an app. By encouraging internet users to download the Starbucks app in exchange for rewards, and then encouraging interaction with the app in every way possible, Starbucks keeps themselves front-of-mind for many customers on a daily basis. And the app is designed to both encourage purchases and streamline the purchasing process.

Like a growing number of brand apps, the Starbucks app allows customers to order ahead, cutting down their wait time when they arrive in the store. Even more important than saving time, having the baristas already know their name and their orders creates the sense that the *brand* knows and cares about them, and gives them some small sense of belonging and importance.

Even more than that, Starbucks has taken the brilliant step of gamifying their loyalty program. When you earn loyalty points by making purchases, you see, you don't *just* get points toward an eventual free coffee or cookie—you also game points in a game of status, where purchasers who spend the most are considered "elite" customers and even given "Starbucks Gold Cards"—gift cards that can be loaded with cash that can only be spent on Starbucks products, but imitate the look, feel, and reward point system of the elite credit cards wielded by the ultra-wealthy.

To keep brand engagement up even when customers aren't looking to spend money or get a caffeine fix, the Starbucks app even incorporates Starbucks-branded games that can be played on your phone.

This complete package of integrated digital and physical spaces and use of in-app purchases to earn physical rewards has allowed the Starbucks experience to grow to encompass far more than coffee and baked goods. Starbucks now supplies its regular customers with a sense of status and identity stemming from their frequent purchases from the brand as well.

CHAPTER 17
HOW TO USE FREEBIES IN MARKETING

ONE FREQUENT POINT of contention in the boardroom is how, and when, to give away free or deeply discounted items. While some decision-makers may have the instinct that people will immediately become lifelong customers when they see how good their free product is, others may feel that giving away free or deeply discounted items lessens the customer's perception of the brand's value. The reality is somewhere in between.

The good news is, there is a lot of data on this topic. We know, for example, that in the restaurant industry it takes about three great experiences to turn a new customer into a lifelong customer. That means that, if you're a restaurant, you need to induce a customer to come through your door—and then deliver a great experience—to obtain hundreds to thousands of dollars in long-term business.

Since each good experience with the brand makes the customer more likely to come back, the value of the giveaways or discounts can be decreased with each customer interaction. This means there is a scientific approach to structuring your discounts and new offers to maximize your return on investment. An optimized progression might look something like this:

1. Through your ads or website, you offer first-time customers

a free dinner for one adult if they attend as part of a party of two or more. You've now gotten two or more new customers through your door with the promise of hearty, free food.

2. You may wish to use a special signaling system, such as use of a different-colored napkin in the table setting, to allow servers to notify the entire restaurant staff that these are first-time customers and need to be treated exceptionally. If the visit goes well, the new customer has a 40% chance of returning.
3. You can increase that chance by having the manager stop by to personally deliver a coupon for $5 off their next visit, along with the manager's personal business card. By forming a one-on-one human connection with the customer and lightly incentivizing a future visit, you make that visit more likely.
4. When customers return and use the $5 off coupon, you may wish to again mark their table for special attention. At the conclusion of this second meal, a second personal visit from the manager to find out how the food was goes a long way toward creating a personal relationship. One final coupon for a free dessert on the customer's next visit will nudge the likelihood of a third visit, occurring just above 42%.
5. If the customer does return for that third meal, there is a 70% chance that they will continue returning in the future. You now have a customer who has been converted from a cold lead into someone with an established habit of dining at your restaurant. It is likely that your ROI will be hundreds to thousands of dollars spent over the course of the customer's lifetime.

Clever use of social media can amplify the impact of such promotions. One approach is to log on to a social media account and privately message the free meal coupon to 100 people who are posting under a relevant local hashtag such as #clevelandohio. This requires no paid advertising, and it feels like a personal gift from the restaurant to the customer.

This approach also targets people who are *already* posting on social media about their experience of the city, and a subtle hint by the manager that the customer may wish to post about their experience with the restaurant wouldn't hurt. In fact, they can amplify their marketing by customers possibly resharing their experience on social media to their followers.

That kind of personal engagement and relationship-building can go a long way to competing with big-box national chains who are unlikely to pay such individual attention to local customers. Global brands may have name recognition, but as we've seen and will continue to see throughout this book, developing a personal relationship between the brand and its customers can allow even higher-priced startups to compete with global chains.

Different statistics for precisely how many interactions are needed to acquire a lifetime customer can be found for different industries. The underlying logic of using freebies and discounts to attract new customers remains the same. By helping customers form a habit of doing business with you, you can strategically improve your return on investment far more effectively than by using freebies with preconditions or strings attached, or by using no freebies at all.

Let's look at some real-world examples of how companies have used giveaways and steep discounts strategically to bring in new customers and cultivate customer loyalty.

CHICK-FIL-A'S FREE SANDWICHES

A free chicken sandwich sounds pretty great, right? Being able to just show up at a restaurant and collect a free sandwich sounds like a good day. That's exactly what Chick-fil-A was banking on when they launched a new promotion to convince people to download their app.

As we covered in the multichannel marketing chapter above, apps are a surprisingly powerful way of cultivating customer loyalty. Apps give companies the ability to send notifications and special offers directly to users' phones, but they also do more than that: they represent an entire brand-specific ecosystem.

Here are some ways apps can be used to encourage repeat sales:

1. Apps can be used to gather personalized data about a customer's past orders, interests, and habits. Chick-fil-A uses individual user data to determine the best times to send personalized notifications upselling customers on their favorite items.

The result is that customers who use Chick-fil-A's app spend more on the restaurant than those who don't. Targeted upselling through the app has increased new product pageviews by 44% and catering orders by 16%.[1]

1. Apps can be used to order food more affordably, or to deliver items not available through multirestaurant hubs like GrubHub or EatStreet—which increases the likelihood that customers will order from your specific brand and not one of the other options offered by those hubs.
2. Apps can be used to rack up loyalty points, which further incentivize customers to order from you, specifically, as often as possible.
3. Apps can be used to deliver coupons and special offers that are precisely designed to encourage purchases highly profitable to your brand, or purchases that may not occur otherwise. Making these offers available *only* to app users can reinforce the incentive for customers to use your loyalty program and direct ordering capabilities.
4. Apps can even be used to deliver in-app games, educational content, and media to help users to form a relationship with your brand.

All of this is why Chick-fil-A's sandwich giveaway was so brilliant. Chick-fil-A would give a free sandwich to absolutely anyone—as long as that person had recently downloaded Chick-fil-A's app to their phone.

It is possible that many users downloaded this app despite never having eaten at Chick-fil-A before, because they wanted a free sandwich. It is possible that slow adopters of technology downloaded the app for the same reason, never intending to use it. It is also possible that many lifelong Chick-fil-A fanatics downloaded the app with the intention of using it to earn loyalty points as they ordered Chick-fil-A on a weekly basis.

In all of these cases, Chick-fil-A wins. They get the opportunity to convert first-time customers into lifelong customers with a great experience, combined with the ultra-convenience of being able to order their food for delivery right from the phone app while being shown a full suite of time-limited promotions. Even app-phobic customers may end up ordering from the app once they see the notifications for the special deals, the loyalty program, and the ultimate convenience of ordering from the app. Lifelong fanatics may order even more often with the constant stream of promotions, plus the convenience of ordering with a few taps on their phone screen.

And Chick-fil-A managed to recruit millions of such customers to their app at the cost of just one free chicken sandwich per person.

Chick-fil-A has continued to leverage their free sandwich giveaways to obtain other strategic gains. As of this writing, a free sandwich is still available to those who take customer satisfaction and desire surveys to help them learn how to more effectively acquire new business and new customers.

No matter what your product or service is, it is likely that you can use an app to strongly increase the frequency of customer purchases. What features are appropriate for you may vary. And of course, all of these apps can offer exclusive special offers and built-in loyalty programs.

Chick-fil-A's use of a free sandwich to inspire app downloads is legendary, but there are other brands who also deserve mentions for their innovative use of discounts and freebies to create massive returns on investment.

STARBUCKS'S HAPPY HOUR

Like Chick-fil-A, Starbucks has had great success using an app to cultivate customer loyalty and increase purchase frequency. Starbucks also uses direct text messages to lower the barrier to users receiving some of their offers and purchases (it's easier to give your phone number than to download an app) and uses both channels to push special offers.

One brilliant use of this direct-to-your-phone communication is Starbucks's "Happy Hour." Though there's no booze involved, the coffee chain will sometimes make special offers or deep discounts available on a very time-restricted schedule, such as offering two-for-the-price-of-one deals during weekday afternoons when their stores are particularly slow.[2]

This deal is clever on multiple levels. By pushing reminders in real time directly to users' phones, Starbucks may induce customers who otherwise would not stop for a 3 p.m. latte to step through the doors to take advantage of the time-limited freebie. By making the deal "two for the price of one," Starbucks also encourages customers to bring a friend in on their mid-afternoon coffee snack, creating the potential to woo first-time or non-habitual customers into a Starbucks habit. Starbucks has even recruited their customers to distribute the free extra drink *for* them. The recipient of the free Starbucks doesn't even necessarily need to expend effort or make the decision to act on the offer themselves.

Or, as Starbucks's website jokes, you could decline to share and drink both drinks yourself. But I think we all know that's a lot of caffeine and steamed milk for 3 p.m. on a Thursday.

Starbucks's innovations using apps and text messaging are many, but their buy-one-get-one-free happy hour is a method that marketers in many industries would do particularly well to learn from. Remember: buy-one-get-one-free simultaneously incentivizes customers to try your product in a time-limited fashion and gives you the potential to reach even more customers by having new or existing customers share your product or service with someone else. You might consider:

- Buy-one-get-one-free for paid consultations or coaching sessions. Customers who may not buy just for themselves may be more incentivized to do so if there's someone in their life who they think could also benefit. The customer gets to give a nice gift, and you get to reach a potential new customer who otherwise may never have considered your services.

- Offering significant freebies around the holidays that would make appropriate standalone gifts for family or friends.
- Targeting buy-one-get-one-free services to address times when business is particularly slow, or to bring in types of customers who are lucrative but difficult to persuade.

It's also worth referencing back here to Mercedes Benz's clever "Take the Wheel" campaign, in which a major freebie was awarded to the Instagram influencer who successfully managed to produce content and leverage their own social network to create the most publicity for Mercedes Benz.

While recruiting that sort of enthusiasm from big name influencers requires a truly big prize, it's a good contrast to the above stories in which relatively low-value items are given away *en masse* in order to cultivate customer loyalty.

If we assume that your industry also operates on some version of the "three times makes a lifelong customer" rule that holds for restaurants, how could you structure giveaways or discounts to successfully attract lifelong customers?

CHAPTER 18
BUILDING RELATIONSHIP THROUGH STORYTELLING

IN OUR LAST CHAPTER, we saw how personal attention and personality can leave customers feeling warm and cared for—an experience that can help your brand stand out from the competition. In this chapter, we'll see how a brand of eyeglasses experienced similar runaway success by showcasing a *story* their customers could relate to.

We all want to do business with people who understand us. We can reasonably expect that those with stories similar to our own will understand our problems better than some megacorporation that has been in the science of hacking sales stats for decades. Let's look at a few examples of brands who overcame apparent disadvantages by identifying with customers through their shared stories.

THE UNDERDOG OF EYEGLASSES

The story of Warby Parker's inception has been the core of their marketing since Day 1. The fact that their company was founded by an ordinary guy who became frustrated upon losing a pair of glasses helped customers everywhere to instantly identify with them.

All my friends who wear glasses have been there at some point. If they haven't lost or broken a pair of glasses, they've had a moment of terror where they *thought* they did. If this happened more than 10 years ago, they knew they were in for a multihundred-dollar purchase if they misplaced or damaged this small and fragile item that they needed to see.

That was the experience of Warby Parker's founder. He happened to be on his way to attend the Wharton School of Business when he lost his glasses. The cost to replace them was so high that he spent a semester without doing so, squinting and complaining the whole time. The business school's encouragement to analyze business models got him thinking. A pair of glasses shouldn't cost $700! In the era of modern technology and online ordering, there was no technical reason at all why an attractive pair of prescription glasses should cost so much. A group of friends he met at Wharton agreed and were puzzled by this problem.[1]

Intrigued, the friends researched why eyeglass prices were so high. What they found shocked them: it turned out that, at the time, nearly all eyeglasses were sold by a single company operating multiple brand names. This company had managed to keep prices artificially high even as the advancing technology pushed the actual cost to manufacture glasses lower and lower.

The friends who founded Warby Parker knew that they could offer much lower prices than the monopoly they'd be competing with. But their competition *was* a corporate giant, and any new brand offering the same product at radically lower prices could expect to be treated with suspicion.

The friends who would go on to found Warby Parker decided to be transparent. They would tell customers exactly what they'd found, and what had motivated them to start a company that could use a modern supply chain to offer glasses at more affordable prices. On top of that, the founders were sure they could do it efficiently enough to offer a free pair of glasses to someone in need for each pair purchased by a customer, while *still* being more affordable than the major eyeglass brands of the time.

The story did more than just explain their low prices: it made it clear to customers that these were average people, just like themselves, who were taking on a national monopoly in order to help average people. They didn't just have a better price point: they had the appeal of *being* the kind of people who most consumers wanted to give money to. And they were smart enough to let consumers know that.

Their story was good enough that it began earning recognition from big names in lifestyle and fashion. Not long after the company's debut, they appeared in both GQ and Vogue. They kept their messaging consistent: "We are average guys who found out that eyewear doesn't have to be expensive. We're making it affordable."

The success of this story was such that, within a few weeks of opening their offerings to the public, Warby Parker was sold out of most of their inventory. They had expected that to take months and found themselves scrambling to meet continued demand.

Warby Parker is proof that the story you tell about your brand is everything. An identical product, sold with a different origin story, might have failed to win the trust and affection of customers. If they had chosen to tell no story at all, a brand claiming to offer a product as sensitive and important as prescription eyewear at such a low price may have been greeted with suspicion. They certainly wouldn't have gotten Vogue and GQ coverage.

Warby Parker has continued to use creative storytelling to gain fame and affection from customers around the world. Recognizing that they started out without the social or cultural capital to match their competitors, they have instead used their underdog status to their advantage in the eyes of the public.

In 2011, for example, Warby Parker wanted to establish themselves as part of the fashion scene by participating in New York's fashion week. However, they lacked the resources and influence to be admitted to the major events of the season. Instead, they planned a secret, guerilla fashion show of their own to take place in a public space the day before fashion week started.

To drive home the everyman character of their company, they selected two tables in the reading room of the New York Public Library for their shoot location. Instead of asking the library for permission for a publicity event, they simply assigned a gaggle of their own employees to occupy the tables. They then invited 40 fashion editors to meet in the Library's front room, cryptically requesting that the invitees keep the event on the down low.[2]

Meanwhile, in the hotel next door, Warby Parker was preparing more than a dozen models to appear wearing signature looks featuring their glasses. At 3:30 p.m., the company's employees vacated their seats and were replaced by the models. The models, all carrying matching books which had been selected for their eye-catching aesthetics, took a seat in this grand, old, respectable public library and began reading with their Warby Parker glasses on.

The invited editors were then ushered in to snap pictures, take notes, and examine the outfits worn by the models. Here were Warby Parker's frames featured in not only a fashion statement, but something of a social statement—this was a place of both venerable, classical architecture and a proud history of accessibility to the everyman. These models were wearing carefully curated cutting-edge fashions but were also engaging in the very practical activity of reading books. They were demonstrating both the style and functionality of the glasses, alongside a deliciously subversive tactic.

It's likely that Warby Parker didn't ask the library for permission to shoot because they were afraid the library would say "no" to hosting an event that could have been completely mobbed by fashion week reporters. But the underground strategy also reinforced the brand's image as a scrappy, subversive entity that could achieve high-end looks using resources that were available to everyday people.

It could be argued, in fact, that the underground approach made *more* of a splash with the target audience than traditional participation in a big fashion week show would have accomplished. While many eyewear customers may feel that the fashion week elites have an air of inaccessible elitism, Warby Parker took the mission of fashion week and outdid the traditional power players precisely by using public resources and flash mob tactics.

In yet another stroke of storytelling genius, Warby Parker created a huge three-day spike in sales by releasing a very unusual annual report. Instead of focusing on their own growth and financials, the company decided this annual report would focus on the customer. The colorful infographics were all about their customers' behavior, ranging from endearingly quirky statistics such as "most popular glasses frames in each U.S. state" and "U.S. states with best and worst eyesight by prescription strength" to statistics about their customers' behavior on social media as far as sharing, hashtagging, and interacting with Warby Parker's posts.

The report was released with an explicit message of gratitude: "We've come so far because of you, thank you so much." Glasses wearers saw themselves in this report and felt pride at having helped the company grow. The report was shared virally, leading to the company's three highest consecutive sales days *ever* up to that point.

Warby Parker is far from the only brand to win through storytelling, but they are a clear illustration of the power of story. The same business model could have had a radically different character and outcome if not for their strong story-driven messaging about their mission and identity. They crafted an identity that customers everywhere could identify with more strongly than with competing brands.

Before you leave this chapter, I'd be out of line if I didn't mention one more Warby Parker stroke of genius in which they managed, as an eyewear brand, to find a creative way to capitalize on the internet's obsession with pets.

One brilliant April Fool's Day, a website called WarbyBarker.com suddenly appeared. The website featured Warby Parker's usual brand of clean, stylish, understated photography of models with dignity and personality wearing Warby Parker glasses. The difference was, these models were dogs.

Warby Barker purported to be the newest offering by Warby Parker: eyewear for your canine friends. Photographs of dignified pugs, intense poodles, and cool bulldogs wearing monocles, glasses, and shades scrolled across the site, which included product pages for a selection of glasses designed for dogs. Attempting to actually order these frames triggered a popup confessing that the "dogocle" was not a real product, but we have to wonder if that's only because Warby Parker couldn't get around the difficulty of sizing for multiple breeds' heads.

WarbyBarker.com quickly started registering over twice the traffic of WarbyParker.com, and was so widely shared on social media that the website is still active to this day.

So, you know. Even if your product isn't *normally* sold to pets, there may be a way to get in on all those dog-driven social media shares.

Who is your target audience? What is their story? What is *your* story? How can you synergize the two, finding the points in your personal and brand story that will invoke affection and a sense of shared identity from your target audience?

THE WORLD'S FAVORITE TRACTOR

Another brand that nails this creatively is that of Mahindra tractors. Mahindra has stood out in recent years for ad campaigns featuring audio and visuals clearly designed to appeal to the quintessentially American image of the rugged farmer—while sporting a noticeably Indian name.

Mahindra can claim the impressive title of the *world's* #1 selling brand of tractors because it originated in India, where it became popular among Indian and Chinese farmers who comprise the two largest agricultural markets on the planet.[3] One can see how this might make penetrating the U.S. market, where farming communities are often proudly patriotic and sometimes harbor skepticism and hostility over the outsourcing of jobs to India and China, difficult.

But Mahindra has made impressive strides by meticulously studying the values and stories of their U.S. target markets—and successfully arguing that Mahindra tractors serve American farmers better than traditionally American brands. Their website heavily features videos of American farmers sharing their own stories of their reluctance to switch to Mahindra tractors, followed by their pleasant surprise at discovering that the tractors were more powerful and easier to use, making the lives of American farmers everywhere easier.

Mahindra tractors do not share an origin story or formative experiences with American farmers. They cannot claim to be American-owned, and they know that it would feel disingenuous to try. Instead, they focus on allowing American farmers to tell their own stories of how their lives have been made easier by these tractors. The fact that Mahindra ranks higher than John Deere in global sales due to its global market doesn't hurt. And who knows—the subtle implication that farmers around the world face the same challenges and share the same values might just help make the world a better place.

To identify the elements that you and your customers' stories have in common, complete the worksheet below or find the printable and downloadable version of it at MiliaMarketing.com / Resources.

CHAPTER 19
FINDING YOUR BRAND STRATEGY

WE HAVE COVERED a huge variety of strategies to hack your brand and compete with industry giants in this book. If your head is spinning a little, don't worry: we've intentionally covered a huge variety of approaches in hopes that two or three of these tips might be applicable to your specific business model.

Remember, there are two key ingredients to brand success: customer conversion, and customer retention.

Excellent customer service and business models that are laser-focused to meet specific needs can allow a brand to cut through the competition, even if options that are more renowned or more cost-effective are already monopolizing market share. But delighting customers alone won't generate sustainable growth: you also have to know the digital marketing algorithms that will put your brand in front of local or global customers as they go about their everyday scrolling.

A friend made an analogy from the book world which I think is apt here. "A poorly written book (a disappointing product or service) can *stop* people from buying. But even the best book in the world won't sell itself if readers don't know that it exists."

To summarize the major points of this book, remember:

1. Strategize before you spend. Don't dump a large budget into an untested initiative. Investment in digital marketing is absolutely crucial—but that doesn't mean *blind* investment. There's a way to test any digital marketing approach on the small scale before authorizing a huge spend.
2. Demand metrics. If your internal or external marketing team is encouraging a course of action, ask to see the details of its conversion rates and ROI. Digital marketing activities are highly trackable, and if your team isn't collecting and analyzing this information, they are likely wasting money.
3. Always be testing. There are countless ways for you to track the outcomes of specific online ad campaigns and promotions. Only by doing this can you learn with certainty which approaches customers respond to. Even advertising experts are often surprised by the results of A/B tests.
4. Have strategic goals. If you are offering a coupon, discount, or freebie, make sure you are using it to incentivize a specific action that you know will translate to positive ROI. Don't just give things away: offer discounts and freebies for strategic goals like turning non-customers into habitual buyers, or incentivizing customers to sign up for your mailing list, direct text messages, or downloads of an app that will keep customers coming back.
5. Remember to wow customers. Low prices, speed, and convenience are not the only ways to set your brand apart. In fact, many case studies suggest that in today's fast-paced marketplace, customers may *prefer* the trust that comes with personal attention and personal relationships over the lowest price or fastest delivery.
6. Don't be afraid to try something new. "The way we've always done it" just doesn't cut it anymore in the rapidly evolving digital age. The good news is, you can try something new without a huge investment using the approaches mentioned above.

In the digital era, the possibilities for how a brand of any size can reach potential customers are literally limitless. The number of venues and services, the technological capabilities of these services, and the number of strategies available make for literally endless ways for you to appear on potential customers' screens.

But that expansiveness itself can be a double-edged sword. Too many businesses throw money into digital marketing with negative or negligible return on investment, because they don't know how to test or optimize their digital marketing approaches.

That's why Milia Marketing exists. We propose strategies specifically crafted for your industry and business model, and conduct A/B testing of ads so you can focus on doing what you do best. We're far from the only outfit offering these services, of course, but we like to believe that we offer one of the best blends of cross-industry expertise and individual attention you'll find.

We hope this book will be useful to your in-house marketing team, or to your own first ventures into digital marketing as an entrepreneur or small-business owner. We know there are so many possible ways for you to reach customers and get a chance to wow them.

And if you ever decide you need a little extra help, we'll be here. We'd love to do business with you.

NOTES

1. UPDATE YOUR STRATEGY FOR SUCCESS

1. Encyclopædia Britannica, inc. (n.d.). *The fastest animals on Earth*. Encyclopædia Britannica. Retrieved February 19, 2022, from https://www.britannica.com/list/the-fastest-animals-on-earth#:~:text=Capable%20of%20going%20from%200,about%2050%20miles%20per%20hour.
2. *December 2017 company of the Month*. Boxed. (n.d.). Retrieved February 19, 2022, from https://www.middlemarketcenter.org/company-of-month/boxed
3. Cepeda, M. (2018, January 22). *If you work for this company, the boss will pay for Your wedding*. Woman's Day. Retrieved February 19, 2022, from https://www.womansday.com/life/work-money/a55650/boxed-boss-employee-wedding/#:~:text=They%20get%20unlimited%20vacation%20time,private%20or%20public%20higher%20education.)

2. DATA, DATA, DATA

1. *4 simple ways to start your revolution*. The DiJulius Group. (2021, February 10). Retrieved February 19, 2022, from https://thedijuliusgroup.com/4-simple-ways-to-start-your-revolution/

4. WHO DOES YOUR CUSTOMER WANT TO BE?

1. Lutz, A. (2015, February 2). *Lululemon calls its ideal customers 'ocean' and 'duke' - here's everything we know about them*. Business Insider. Retrieved January 27, 2022, from https://www.businessinsider.com/lululemon-idea-customers-ocean-and-duke-2015-2

5. YOUR CUSTOMER JOURNEY MAP

1. *Customer and target audience insights*. Long & Short of It. (n.d.). Retrieved February 19, 2022, from https://www.lasoi.com/customer-insights

6. HOW DO YOU KNOW IF YOUR MARKETING IS BAD?

1. *Call Tracking & Marketing Analytics Software*. CallRail. (n.d.). Retrieved February 19, 2022, from https://www.callrail.com/

8. THE ENORMOUS POWER OF TINY CHANGES

1. *Online leatherworks*. Tlusty & Co. Retrieved February 19, 2022, from https://www.tlustyco.com/
2. Linowski, J. (n.d.). *Netflix designs their button a little too big*. GoodUI. Retrieved February 14, 2022, from https://goodui.org/leaks/netflix-designs-their-button-a-little-too-big/
3. Wolverton, Troy (September 18, 2000). "Apple licenses Amazon's 1-Click". CNET News.com. Archived from the original on February 3, 2009. Retrieved November 19, 2008.

10. GIVE THEM A GREAT EXPERIENCE

1. Nadams. (2016, May 4). *Cavs and Budweiser team up to bring virtual reality experience*. Cleveland Cavaliers. Retrieved February 19, 2022, from https://www.nba.com/cavaliers/releases/vr-160504
2. Wilson, M. (2022, January 6). *Nike raises its retail game*. Chain Store Age. Retrieved February 19, 2022, from https://chainstoreage.com/news/nike-raises-its-retail-game

13. GO VIRAL WITH SHARING INCENTIVES

1. Pulizzi, J. (2021, September 28). *Onlyfans' content ban: Don't build on rented land*. The Tilt. Retrieved February 19, 2022, from https://www.thetilt.com/audience/dont-build-on-rented-land
2. *Mercedes-Benz take the wheel*. James, Nicole. Retrieved February 19, 2022, from http://www.nicolejames.nyc/mercedesbenz-take-the-wheel
3. *Doubletree Cookies*. DoubleTree Cookie. (n.d.). Retrieved February 19, 2022, from https://www.doubletreecookies.com/
4. Stevenson, S. (2004, February 23). *The Singing Quiznos Rodents, explained*. Slate Magazine. Retrieved February 19, 2022, from https://slate.com/business/2004/02/the-singing-quiznos-rodents-explained.html
5. Larson, S. (2021, December 28). *How restaurants get michelin stars: A brief history of the michelin guide*. Escoffier. Retrieved February 19, 2022, from https://www.escoffier.edu/blog/world-food-drink/a-brief-history-of-the-michelin-guide/

14. CONNECT AUTHENTICALLY

1. *Real marketing*. Marketing Examples. Retrieved February 19, 2022, from https://marketingexamples.com/brand/real

15. WHAT'S YOUR RETURN ON EXPERIENCE?

1. *Client success*. The DiJulius Group. (2022, February 10). Retrieved February 19, 2022, from https://thedijuliusgroup.com/client-success/

17. HOW TO USE FREEBIES IN MARKETING

1. *Chick-fil-A*. Case Study: Chick-Fil-A Increases Online Revenue Through Customer Engagement & Loyalty. Retrieved February 20, 2022, from https://www.sitecore.com/customers/retail/chick-fil-a
2. *Starbucks® happy hour: Starbucks Coffee Company*. Starbucks® Happy Hour: Starbucks Coffee Company. Retrieved February 20, 2022, from https://www.starbucks.com/rewards/happy-hour/

18. BUILDING RELATIONSHIP THROUGH STORYTELLING

1. *History*. Warby Parker. Retrieved February 20, 2022, from https://www.warbyparker.com/history
2. Lo, D. (2011, September 7). *Warby Parker's guerilla eyewear show at the NY Public Library*. Racked. Retrieved February 20, 2022, from https://www.racked.com/2011/9/7/7752109/warby-parkers-guerilla-eyewear-show-at-the-ny-public-library
3. Admin. (2022, February 12). *Top 10 tractor companies in the world - tractor list 2022*. TractorJunction. Retrieved February 20, 2022, from https://www.tractorjunction.com/blog/top-10-tractor-companies-in-the-world-tractor-list/

ABOUT THE AUTHOR

Anthony Milia is the owner and founder of the award-winning firm Milia Marketing. He's proud to have helped countless companies increase their traffic and revenue, build solid customer foundations, and take their business to the next level. And now he's ready to assist you. In "Marketing Magnifier," Milia seeks to help readers grow their customer base and their revenue by asking simple questions which are often overlooked. His goal is to demystify marketing and counter common misconceptions which business owners can easily fall prey to. Anthony currently resides in Cleveland, OH with his indispensable counterpart. When he's not working, he enjoys travel, going on adventures, hiking in the great outdoors, and reading. With a goal of helping more businesses thrive, Anthony welcomes anyone to reach out to him at: anthony@miliamarketing.com.

twitter.com/anthonymilia

instagram.com/anthonymilia

linkedin.com/in/anthonymilia

facebook.com/miliamarketing

For permission to quote, book a speaking engagement, or order books in bulk, write to the publisher with the subject line "Attention: Permissions Coordinator," at the address below:

anthony@miliamarketing.com

Special discounts are available on quantity purchases for bookstores, corporations, associations, and others. For details, contact the publisher at the address above.

DISCLAIMER

This book is designed to share general information about the marketing world for informational purposes. It is not designed to provide specific advice for any particular business. As we will discuss in the pages to come, every business's product and target audience are different. The task of the business owner is to ask the right questions to determine the best way of reaching *their* customers.

For that reason, the author and publisher make no guarantees about the results of using marketing strategies contained in this book. Seeking personalized expert advice for your business is always recommended when creating a marketing strategy.

The author hopes that the information contained within this book may assist you in knowing the right questions to ask.

Made in United States
Cleveland, OH
04 November 2026

47642873R00103